Oxford Discover

Student Book 5

Kenna Bourke

OXFORD
UNIVERSITY PRESS

Scope and Sequence

UNIT	READING	VOCABULARY	GRAMMAR
	BIG QUESTION 1	**Why do we protect animals?** Social Studies: History	
1 Page 6	**Dreaming of Dodos** Fantasy (Fiction) **Reading Strategy** Author's Purpose	**Reading Text Words** *dodo, elephant bird, quagga, sea wolf, woolly mammoth, extinct, survive, exploit, endangered, habitat, species, sanctuary* **Words in Context** *existed, eventually, mammals, suffered, atmosphere, rare* **Word Study** Suffix *-able*	**Present Perfect and Present Perfect Continuous** Affirmative and negative statements, questions *I have read books about dodos.* *I have been reading this book for an hour.*
2 Page 16	**Save Our Tigers!** Article (Nonfiction) **Reading Strategy** Monitor and Clarify	**Reading Text Words** *diverse, identify, tracker, protect, naturalist, poaching, damaged, conservation, preservation, inspire, population, reserve* **Words in Context** *jungles, wildlife, hunter, injuries, mission, national park* **Word Study** Synonyms	**Review of Tenses** Affirmative and negative statements, *has* and *have* statements *People have cleared forests to grow crops.* *The animals' habitat has suffered.*
	BIG QUESTION 2	**What are teeth for?** Life Science	
3 Page 26	**"The Cavity" and "Have You Any Idea?"** Poems (Fiction) **Reading Strategy** Looking for Sensory Details	**Reading Text Words** *incisor, canine, molar, carnivore, herbivore, omnivore, slice, grip, crush, cavity, gums, jaw* **Words in Context** *detective, dental, gravity, filling, treat, munch* **Word Study** Prefix *in-*	**Modals of Ability** Past, present, and future statements, negative statements *I could read by the time I was four.* *Next year, I will be able to ride my bike to school.* *I won't be able to drive a car.*
4 Page 36	**Teeth: Not Just for Eating** Informational Text (Nonfiction) **Reading Strategy** Using Visuals	**Reading Text Words** *fang, tusk, venom, shelter, dam, prey, gnaw, pierce, fend off, wear down, lap up, create* **Words in Context** *powerful, intruders, supply, seal, toppling, lodge* **Word Study** Suffix *-ment*	**Modals of Certainty** Affirmative and negative statements, questions *It must be a prosimian. It has comb-like lower teeth.* *That can't be a spider! It only has four legs.*
	BIG QUESTION 3	**Why are wheels important?** Social Studies: History	
5 Page 46	**A Revolution in History** Informational Text (Nonfiction) **Reading Strategy** Re-reading	**Reading Text Words** *transportation, transfer, haul, axle, rotate, spoke, rim, traction, gear, grind, technology, rod* **Words in Context** *platform, vehicle, durable, mill, mechanical, inspiring* **Word Study** Compound Nouns	**Future with *Will* and *Going to*** Affirmative statements *The sun will rise at 6:05 tomorrow.* *I'm going to visit my uncle next week.*
6 Page 56	**Planet SinRota** Science Fiction (Fiction) **Reading Strategy** Drawing Conclusions	**Reading Text Words** *obedient, fortunate, tedious, exciting, fragile, determined, daring, foolish, thrilling, courageous, risky, fascinated* **Words in Context** *settlement, longed for, blurry, figures, propelling, adjusted* **Word Study** Prefix *mis-*	**Future with Present Continuous** Affirmative and negative statements, questions and short answers *We are meeting our friends at 2:00 on Friday.* *The moon will rise at ten o'clock tonight.* *I'm going to take a music class next year.*
	BIG QUESTION 4	**How do animals communicate?** Life Science	
7 Page 68	**Magdi and the Dolphin** Narrative Fiction (Fiction) **Reading Strategy** Character	**Reading Text Words** *race, drift, glide, wade, paddle, dive, splash, propel, float, sprint, jog, plod* **Words in Context** *fishing rod, chuckled, hook, beamed, paddles, grinning* **Word Study** Letter Combination *-gh*	**Reported Speech with *Said That*** Affirmative and negative statements *"It's a beautiful day," said Magdi.* *Magdi said that it was a beautiful day.*
8 Page 78	**Chatterboxes** Article (Nonfiction) **Reading Strategy** Asking Questions	**Reading Text Words** *communicative, locate, collaborate, imitate, behave, indicate, attract, threaten, defend, approach, express, produce* **Words in Context** *underwater, decibels, territory, alarm, signals, difficulty* **Word Study** Suffix *-ion*	**Reported Speech with *Told* or *Asked*** Affirmative statements *He told us that Kanzi was learning new things every day.* *A classmate asked the scientist what Kanzi was learning.*

Finn Sonya Charlie April

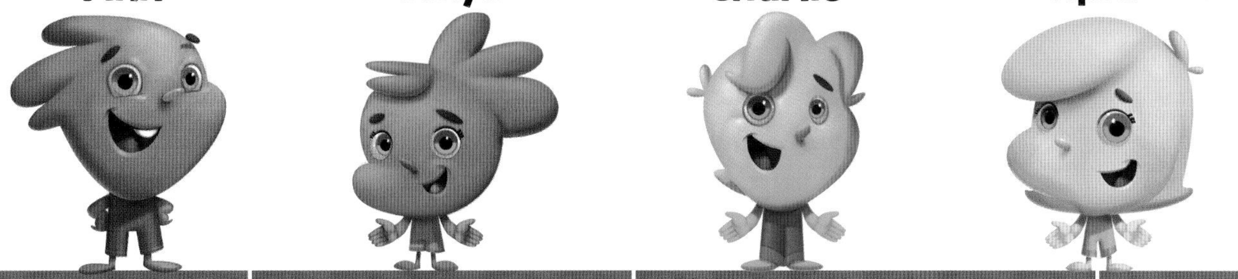

LISTENING	SPEAKING	WRITING	WRAP UP
The Goliath Frog A conversation about the largest frog in the world **Listening Strategy** Listening for main idea	**Talking About an Opinion** *In my opinion, the most interesting animal is the Goliath frog.*	**Sentence Fragments** *Zebras on grass, twigs, and leaves.* *Zebras survive on grass, twigs, and leaves.* **Writing Practice** Write about animals (Workbook)	• **Writing** Write a persuasive e-mail (Workbook) • **Presentation** Share your e-mail with the class • **Review** Units 1 and 2 (Workbook) Big Question 1 Review
Panda Bears An interview about pandas **Listening Strategy** Listening for details	**Giving Reasons** *I think tigers will survive.* *Why do you say that?* *People will help tigers because ...*	**Irregular Past Verbs** *She caught a cold.* **Writing Practice** Write about animals you've studied (Workbook)	
Caring for Your Teeth Instructions for brushing your teeth **Listening Strategy** Listening for instructions	**Talking about Teeth** *I think it is important to take care of your teeth.* *I agree. We should brush our teeth every day.*	**Adjective + Preposition** *I'm interested in sports.* **Writing Practice** Write about your interests when you were little and your interests now (WB)	• **Writing** Write a report (WB) • **Presentation** Share your report with the class • **Review** Units 3 and 4 (WB) Big Question 2 Review
Killer Whales A radio interview with an expert on killer whales **Listening Strategy** Listening for details	**Comparing Things** *I think beavers are more interesting than walruses because they build homes.*	**Parallel Structure with *-ing*** *Wei enjoys playing, singing, and acting.* **Writing Practice** Write about what you or someone you know likes to do (WB)	
The Printing Press A speaker discusses the importance of wheels in the creation of books **Listening Strategy** Listening for main idea	**Planning a Trip** *We're going to France. First, we'll take the bus to the airport.*	**Verb + Infinitive** *I agreed to go with him.* **Writing Practice** Write about plans with friends and family (WB)	• **Writing** Write an opinion essay (WB) • **Presentation** Share your opinion essay with the class • **Review** Units 5 and 6 (WB) Big Question 3 Review
Guessing Game One child describes an object, and the other guesses what it is **Listening Strategy** Listening for details	**Giving Advice** *I missed the bus. What should I do?* *You should ask your dad to give you a ride.*	**More Irregular Verbs** *become → became* **Writing Practice** Write about what you wanted to be when you were a child and what you want to be now (WB)	**Testing Practice 1**
Humpback Whales An interview with an expert on the singing of humpback whales **Listening Strategy** Listening for details	**Asking for Clarification** *When I was five, I fell out of a tree.* *How did that happen?*	**Commas and Semicolons** *We had a storm last night, but it cleared up.* *We had a storm last night; it cleared up.* **Writing Practice** Write about how an animal communicates (WB)	• **Writing** Write a descriptive essay (WB) • **Presentation** Share your descriptive essay with the class • **Review** Units 7 and 8 (WB) Big Question 4 Review
Echo the Elephant An interview with an elephant expert **Listening Strategy** Listening for details	**Summarizing What You've Learned** *What did you learn about bees?* *I learned that honeybees communicate by dancing.*	**Pronoun Agreement** *The girl is watching a movie. She likes it.* **Writing Practice** Write about a place you have seen animals (WB)	

LISTENING	SPEAKING	WRITING	WRAP UP
History			
The Olympic Games A conversation about Greece and the Olympics **Listening Strategy** Listening for facts	**Using Question Words** What invention do you think is important?	**Using Parentheses** *Jorge (Luke's friend) is coming over to our house tonight.* **Writing Practice** Write about something you've learned (WB)	• **Writing** Write a travel brochure (WB) • **Presentation** Share your travel brochure with the class • **Review** Units 9 and 10 (WB) Big Question 5 Review
The Invention of the Umbrella A conversation about umbrellas **Listening Strategy** Listening for details	**Making Suggestions** How about we study for the test together?	**Giving Examples** *There are many ways to keep fit,* for example, *swimming, jogging, or playing a sport.* **Writing Practice** Write about what different cultures give to the world (WB)	
Mountain Climate A lecture about plants, animals, and weather in the mountains **Listening Strategy** Listening for key words	**Interviewing** Where would you like to live? I'd like to live at the top of the mountain.	**Colons** *We bought food for the party: cake, ice cream, and chips.* **Writing Practice** Write about something you've learned this week (WB)	• **Writing** Write a story (WB) • **Presentation** Share your story with the class • **Review** Units 11 and 12 (WB) Big Question 6 Review
Weather Report A weather reporter gives the forecast **Listening Strategy** Listening for gist	**Asking for Advice** I'm going to the mountains. Do you think I should bring a coat?	**Irregular Past Participles** *He* chose *to go out in the snowstorm.* **Writing Practice** Write about something you've made, written, or drawn (WB)	**Testing Practice 2**
Banking and Money A conversation about saving, investing, spending, and donating **Listening Strategy** Listening for details	**Future Plans** What do you want right now? Now, I want to save for a new soccer ball.	**Adverbs of Degree** *Pia finished her work* extremely *quickly.* *These noodles are* absolutely *delicious!* **Writing Practice** Write about a place you've visited (WB)	• **Writing** Write a summary (WB) • **Presentation** Share your summary with the class • **Review** Units 13 and 14 (WB) Big Question 7 Review
If I Had a Lot of Money A survey about how kids would spend money **Listening Strategy** Listening for speakers	**Talking about Money** Who would you help? I would donate the money to a hospital.	**Similes** *It's* as *cold* as *ice in here!* *My bedroom is* like *a nest, all cozy and warm.* **Writing Practice** Write about your home, family, or friends (WB)	
Ramiro the Drummer An interview with a young musician **Listening Strategy** Listening for details	**Explaining Your Opinions** I think art is the most important form of self-expression. Why do you say that? I think it's important because it will last for many years.	**Quantifiers** *Most of my friends live in an apartment.* **Writing Practice** Write about your city or neighborhood (WB)	• **Writing** Write a scene from a play (WB) • **Presentation** Perform your scene for the class • **Review** Units 15 and 16 (WB) Big Question 8 Review
Dancing A dancer's description of why she enjoys dancing **Listening Strategy** Listening for details	**Expressing Thanks** Please share this candy with me. Thanks so much!	**Semicolons** *I saw an artist on TV; she won a prize.* **Writing Practice** Write about how you like to express yourself (WB)	
Life in a Lighthouse An interview with a lighthouse keeper **Listening Strategy** Listening for details	**Giving Reasons** I'd like to live in an apartment. Why? I think it's because I want to live in a city.	**Run-On Sentences** *I don't like tall buildings they scare me.* *I don't like tall buildings because they scare me.* **Writing Practice** Write about interesting buildings you've seen (WB)	• **Writing** Write a magazine article (WB) • **Presentation** Share your magazine article with the class • **Review** Units 17 and 18 (WB) Big Question 9 Review
Japanese Homes A description of Japanese traditional homes **Listening Strategy** Listening for main idea	**Accepting or Refusing Invitations** Let's play tennis on Thursday, OK? I'm sorry. I'm busy that day.	**Order of Adjectives** *Look at that* horrible, big, black *cloud.* **Writing Practice** Write about a building, sculpture, or object from another country (WB)	**Testing Practice 3**

In units **1** and **2** you will:

WATCH
a video about animals.

LEARN
why animals are important to us.

READ
about animals and people who help them.

WRITE a persuasive e-mail.

PRESENT your e-mail to the class.

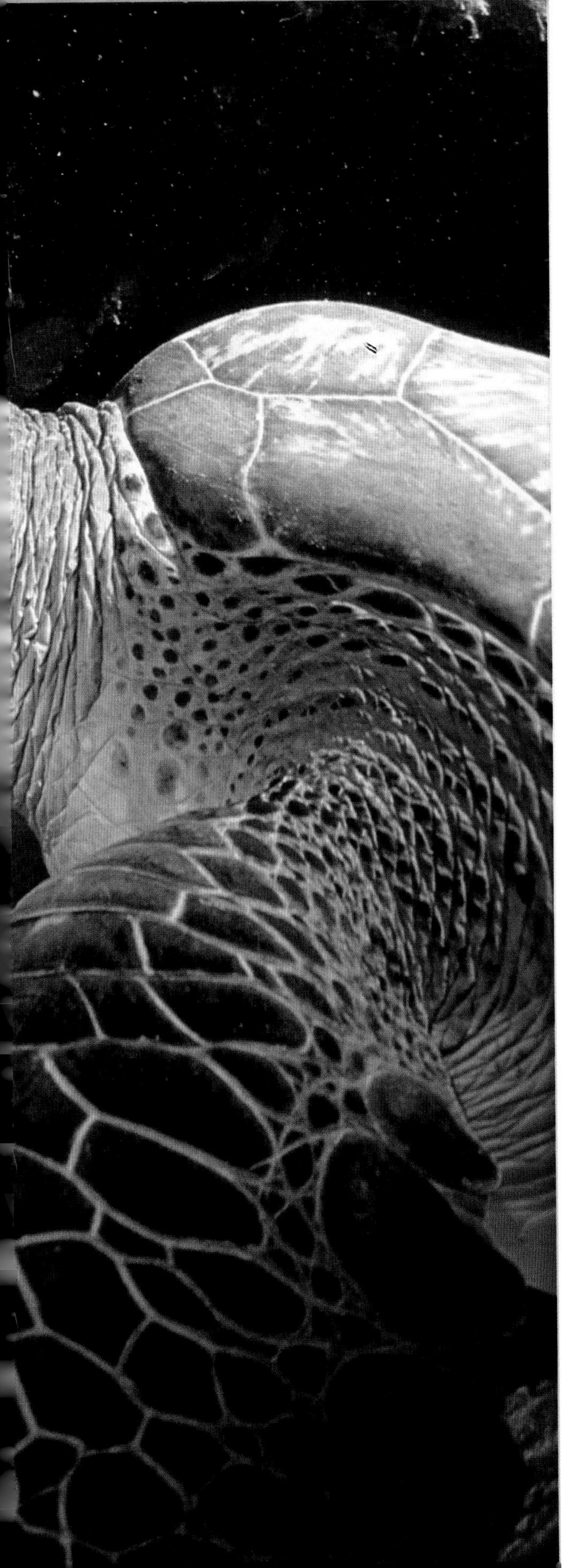

BIG QUESTION 1

Why do we protect animals?

A **Watch the video. Then talk about it with your partner.**

B **Look at the picture and discuss it with your class.**

1 What do you think the diver is doing?
2 What kind of animal is this? Is it afraid?

C **Think and answer the questions.**

1 Can you think of some animals that are in danger?
2 What do you know about these animals?
3 Why are these animals in danger?
4 Why is it important to help these animals?

D **Discuss this topic with your class. Fill out the Big Question Chart.**

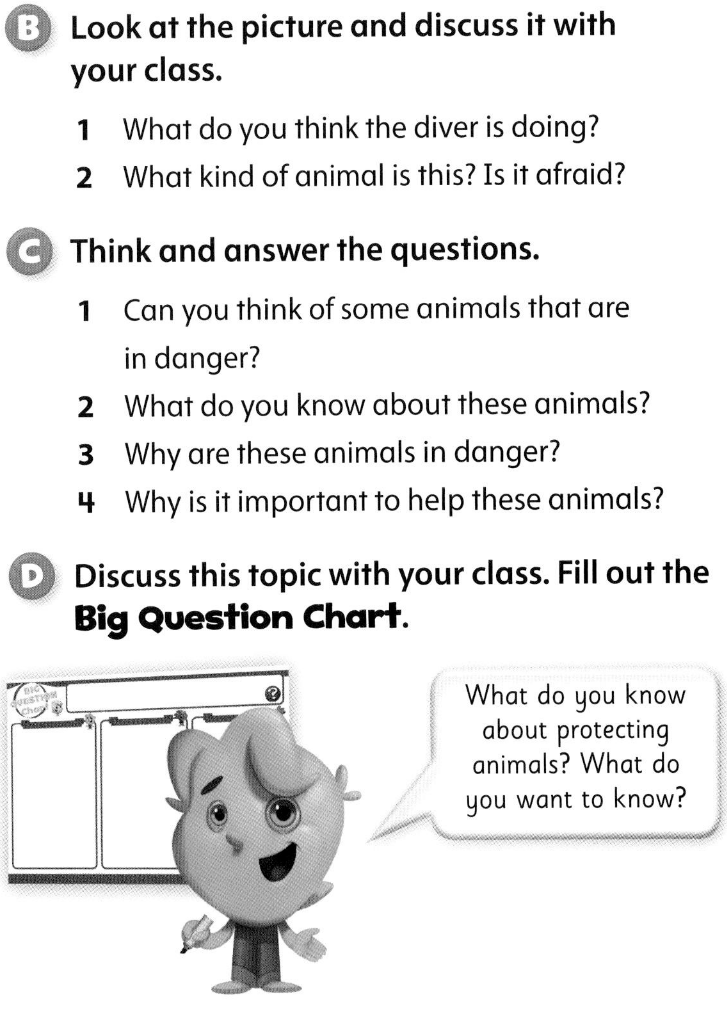

UNIT 1 Get Ready

Words

A Listen and say the words. Then read and listen to the sentences. 1•02

dodo	elephant bird	quagga	sea wolf	woolly mammoth	extinct
survive	exploit	endangered	habitat	species	sanctuary

1 **Dodos** were birds that lived a long time ago and couldn't fly.
2 **Elephant birds** were very tall and too heavy to fly.
3 **Quaggas** looked like zebras with stripes only on the fronts of their bodies.
4 **Sea wolves** lived in the ocean and had flippers.
5 **Woolly mammoths** were related to elephants.
6 Dodos are **extinct**. None are alive today.
7 Tigers still **survive** today, even though there are fewer of them.
8 Some people unfairly **exploit** animals for their fur.
9 Polar bears are in danger of becoming extinct. They are **endangered** animals.
10 African lions live in the grasslands. It is their **habitat**.
11 Many different **species** of birds live in nature reserves.
12 Endangered animals can live safely in **sanctuaries**.

B Circle the one that doesn't belong.

1	woolly mammoth	elephant bird	dodo	human
2	die	survive	exist	live
3	extinct	dead	alive	disappeared
4	take advantage	misuse	respect	exploit
5	endangered	safe	threatened	at risk
6	habitat	home	quagga	sanctuary

C Circle the correct answer.

1 Which animal was a bird that couldn't fly?
quagga sea wolf species elephant bird

2 Which animal was related to an elephant?
dodo elephant bird quagga woolly mammoth

3 Which animal was similar to a zebra?
quagga tiger sea wolf dodo

Before You Read

Think **Answer the questions.**

1 Why are animals important to us?
2 Do you know of any endangered animals?

D **Learn** Author's Purpose

When you read, think about why the author wrote the story.

- How does the author want you to feel?
- What does the author want you to learn?
- How does the author feel about the subject?

Read the paragraphs. Check (✓) what the author wants you to do.

1

Your city needs your help. What could you do to help? Your class could start a clean-up project near your school.

☐ have fun ☐ take action ☐ learn

2

All animals need water. Some animals drink from rivers. Other animals drink from rainwater that has landed on leaves. Animals live where they can find water.

☐ have fun ☐ take action ☐ learn

3

"Miko, your father and I are worried about you," said Miko's mother. "You seem to be asleep most of the time."

"Zzzzzz," snored Miko the sloth.

☐ have fun ☐ take action ☐ learn

E **Words in Context** **Scan the story on pages 10–11 and circle these words. As you read, try to guess what the words mean.**

existed eventually mammals suffered atmosphere rare

F **Turn to pages 10–11 again. Look at the pictures and the title. What do you think the story is about? Could it happen in real life?**

PREVIEW

Dreaming of Dodos

In this *fantasy* story, a girl named Mina has a dream about some animals that no longer exist. A fantasy is a type of story about characters and events that could not happen in real life. As you read, think about why the author wrote the story.

Read 1·03

Dreaming of Dodos

Mina was in bed, feeling sleepy. She read the first few words of her book.

"The dodo was a bird that couldn't fly. ..."

Whoosh! The window flew wide open. Mina sat up, and through the window she saw a dodo, a real live dodo, right there in her yard!

"I existed over four hundred years ago," the dodo said. "But then terrible things happened. Sailors arrived. They cut down the forests, so there was nothing for us to eat, and they had cats that killed us. Dodos didn't survive. We all died."

The dodo made a sniffing noise and sat down.

There was a sound of hooves, and into the yard galloped a quagga, missing the dodo's head by a centimeter.

"I existed 150 years ago," said the quagga, with a tear in its eye. "Quaggas were a species of zebra, but hunters killed us and made our skins into bags, and farmers ate us. These humans exploited us. Eventually, we all became extinct."

The quagga stood by Mina's swing, swishing its tail.

Soon came a sound of water gushing and a flip-flap of flippers. From the bottom of Mina's pool emerged a sea wolf. It looked like a big seal.

"I've been looking for you!" said the sea wolf to the dodo. "Sea wolves haven't existed for almost 70 years."

"Why's that?" asked the dodo.

The sea wolf flopped out of the pool. A puddle of water spread across the grass.

"We were hunted by explorers, fishermen, and hunters who killed and ate us. They made shoes and boots from our skin, and used our fat to cook with. That's why!"

"I'm very sorry," said the dodo. The dodo felt bad that

Think
How does the author want you to feel?

these sea mammals had suffered so much.

Suddenly, a crashing noise made Mina jump. There at the gate was a woolly mammoth. With one big push, it stumbled into the yard.

"Sorry about the noise," it said. "I've been looking for you! I lived thousands of years ago, but now I'm extinct."

"Why's that?" asked the quagga.

"No one is sure," replied the mammoth. "Scientists think the weather changed, changing our habitat. We ate grass, but as the atmosphere grew warmer, forests spread and there was less grass to eat."

Mina heard wings flapping. Seconds later, an elephant bird came crashing through the trees and landed beside the pool, splashing water over the dodo.

"I weigh half a ton," the elephant bird said proudly. "I'm the heaviest bird that's ever existed. You could make 30 omelets from one of my eggs! But I've been extinct for over a thousand years."

Well, the animals all looked miserable, but before they had time to say another word, a tiger came roaring in.

"Ah-hah!" it said, peering around with its bright, fiery eyes. "I have many friends here."

"Are you extinct, too?" asked the elephant bird.

"Not yet," replied the tiger, flashing its shiny teeth. "But I'm rare and endangered! Tigers are lucky. They have sanctuaries where they can live."

The dodo, the quagga, the sea wolf, the woolly mammoth, and the elephant bird all stared at the tiger. "Sanctuaries?" they asked.

"Yes, sanctuaries," replied the tiger. "They are places where no one can hurt you."

"What a great idea!" thought Mina. "Maybe if we have sanctuaries, fewer animals will become extinct."

The window blew shut, and Mina woke up with a start. There was no one and nothing to see, except the book by her bed.

Think

What does the author want you to learn?

Understand

Comprehension

Think What did you like about "Dreaming of Dodos"? Tell your partner two things you liked about the story.

A As a class, discuss the author's purpose for writing "Dreaming of Dodos." Did the author want you to have fun, take action, or learn something?

B Circle the correct answer.

1 Mina was ______
- **a** in the yard, playing with extinct animals.
- **b** in bed, reading about endangered animals.
- **c** in bed, reading about extinct animals.
- **d** at the gate, letting in the animals.

2 Tigers are lucky because ______
- **a** they can live in sanctuaries.
- **b** they have big, shiny teeth.
- **c** they can eat large animals.
- **d** they can live on safe islands.

3 Sailors cut down the forests ______
- **a** and there was nothing for dodos to eat.
- **b** to let cats eat all the food.
- **c** so dodos had to move to another country.
- **d** and put all the dodos on their ships.

4 The author wanted readers to ______
- **a** remember every word of the story.
- **b** learn about extinct animals.
- **c** dream about dodos.
- **d** memorize facts about animals.

C **Words in Context** Look again at the words you circled in the story. Write them in the correct places in the paragraph.

Many ______ (1), as well as many marine animals and birds that ______ (2) long ago, were unfairly exploited by humans. ______ (3), some of these animals died out. Even today, many animals face the threat of extinction. Pandas, for example, are increasingly ______ (4) in the wild. Some of these animals have ______ (5) from the fact that our ______ (6) has become warmer. Others have been hunted and killed.

Workbook Grammar
pages 6–7

Grammar in Use

D **Listen and read along. Then answer the questions.** 1•04

1 Is Finn painting now? Yes No

2 Has Charlie painted anything before? Yes No

E **Learn Grammar** **Present Perfect and Present Perfect Continuous**

Use the **present perfect** to say what you've done in your life up to now.

I have read books about dodos. (I read these books in the past.)

Use the **present perfect continuous** to say that you started doing something in the past and you're still doing it now.

I have been reading this book for an hour. (I'm still reading it.)

Read the sentences. Which sentences say that the action is still happening?

1 They've been playing basketball since three o'clock.
2 We've read books about mountains and oceans.
3 I haven't eaten my breakfast.
4 Maria and I have been doing our homework for an hour.
5 Have you been to the new store yet?
6 I've been learning English for four years.

F **Work with your partner. Take turns stating two facts about you using the present perfect and the present perfect continuous.**

Communicate

Listening

Think What are some reasons that people hunt animals?

A Listen. What is the main idea the speaker wants you to learn about Goliath frogs? 1•05

B Listen again. Then check (✓) the correct box. 1•06

1	Goliath frogs can grow up to …	☐ 33 meters.	☐ 33 centimeters.
2	They can weigh as much as a …	☐ baby.	☐ cat.
3	Goliath frogs live in …	☐ Asia.	☐ Africa.
4	Goliath frogs have existed for …	☐ 250 million years.	☐ 25 thousand years.
5	People hunt these frogs for …	☐ food.	☐ their skin.
6	Some people keep Goliath frogs …	☐ as pets.	☐ as decorations.

Speaking 1•07

C **Learn** Talking About an Opinion

When you give an opinion, it's a good idea to give reasons. Use **because**, **I say that because**, or **in my experience**. To ask someone reasons, use **Why do you say that?** or **Why do you think that?**

Work with your partner. Choose a topic and take turns giving and asking about your opinions.

- **most interesting animal**
- **most dangerous animal**
- **most endangered animal**
- **most important animal to protect**

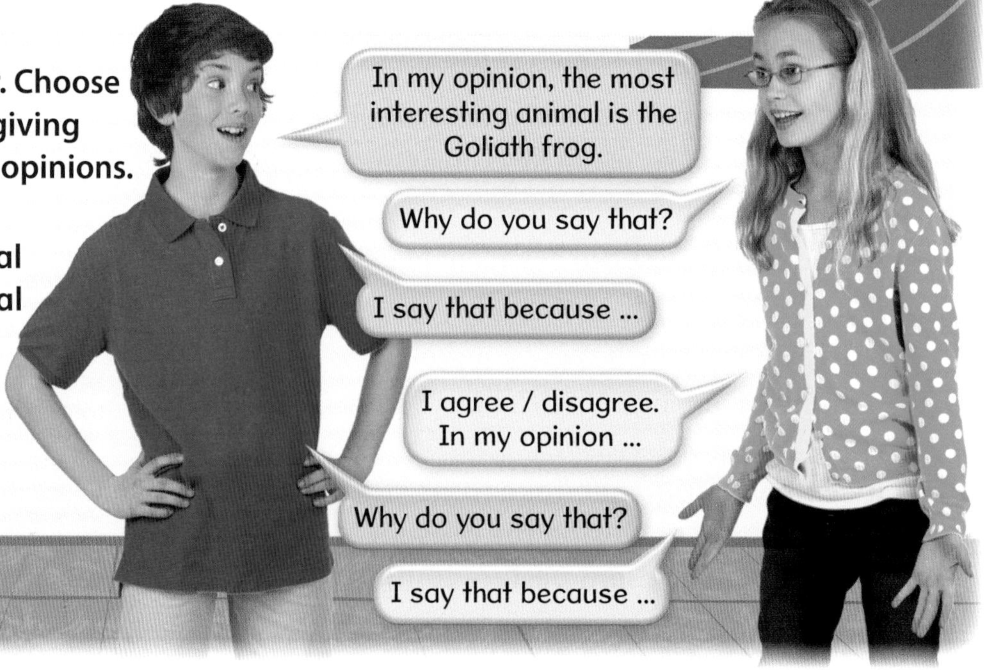

Word Study

D **Learn** Suffix *-able*

Remember: A suffix is added to the end of a word. The suffix -able is sometimes added to a noun or a verb to make it an adjective.

comfort + able = comfortable

I enjoy the comfort of my home. My home Is very comfortable.

Listen and say the words. Look them up in the dictionary. Write the words by adding *-able*. If a noun or verb ends in an *e* cross out the last letter. 1•08 A-Z page 192

1 depend ________	**2** excite ________	**3** prevent ________	**4** comfort ________
5 adjust ________	**6** adore ________	**7** solve ________	**8** avoid ________

Writing Study

E **Learn** Sentence Fragments

A sentence fragment is missing a subject or a verb.

Zebras on grass, twigs, and leaves.

Fix a sentence fragment by adding a subject or a verb.

Zebras survive on grass, twigs, and leaves.

Write S for sentence or F for fragment.

1 Running as fast as possible. ________

2 Small numbers of pandas live in the wild. ________

3 Not in the ocean, however. ________

4 No one knows where they come from. ________

Write Now practice writing in the **Workbook.** page 9

BIG QUESTION 1

Why do we protect animals?

The dodo and his friends were sad because they weren't protected.

What are some ways that we protect animals?

UNIT 2 Get Ready

Words

A Listen and say the words. Then read and listen to the sentences. 1•09

diverse | identify | tracker | protect | naturalist | poaching
damaged | conservation | preservation | inspire | population | reserve

1 Wildlife in the mountains is **diverse**. There are many kinds of animals.
2 Can you **identify** the animal in this picture?
3 A **tracker** is trained to find animals.
4 We need to **protect** our forests so animals can survive there.
5 **Naturalists** study living things.
6 **Poaching** is illegal. A poacher kills animals.
7 When a habitat is **damaged**, animals can't live there.
8 **Conservation** of animals' habitats is important for their survival.
9 Sanctuaries help the **preservation** of endangered animals.
10 The beauty of the mountains often **inspires** artists to paint.
11 The **population** of mountain gorillas has recently gone down.
12 Animals that are endangered sometimes live in a **reserve**.

B Write each word in the correct column.

preservation protect tracker conservation identify naturalist inspire

People's Jobs	Good Ideas	Actions
___	___	___
___	___	___
___	___	___
___	___	___

C Work with your partner to complete the sentences.

1 The number of animals in a group is the ______________.
2 When a habitat is ______________, animals can't live there.
3 A ______________ is a place for endangered animals to be safe.
4 There are lots of species here. There's a ______________ group.

diverse
population
damaged
reserve

Before You Read

Think Answer the questions.

1 What do you know about tigers?
2 Why do we protect them?

D **Learn** Monitor and Clarify

Make sure you understand what you're reading.

- Monitor your understanding. Good readers re-read sentences they don't understand.
- Read ahead. You can find new clues to help you understand what you're reading.
- Look at the pictures, charts, and diagrams. They may clarify what you're reading.

Read the paragraph about sloths. Answer the questions.

Sloths have existed for about 60 million years. They live in the rainforests of South and Central America. They live in trees, where they hang upside down, and they rarely visit the ground. There are several species of sloths. Some have three toes and some have two toes. They mostly eat insects, small birds, and leaves.

1 Did you re-read sentences you didn't understand?
2 Did you read ahead?
3 Did the picture help clarify what you read?

E **Words in Context** **Scan the article on pages 18–19 and circle these words. As you read, try to guess what the words mean.**

jungles **wildlife** **hunter** **injuries** **mission** **national park**

F **Look at the article on pages 18–19.**

1 How many sections are there? Read the titles.
2 Write down two things you think the article is about.

PREVIEW

SAVE OUR TIGERS!

In this *article*, you will learn about India, tigers, and a man who helped save tigers.

Part of the article is *biographical*. A biography gives information and facts about a person. As you read, monitor your understanding of the article.

Social Studies: History

Read 1•10

SAVE OUR TIGERS!

The Foothills of the Himalayas

The Himalayas are the highest range of mountains on Earth. Below this range, there are foothills containing jungles, forests, rivers, and lakes. These hills once provided a home to many diverse types of wildlife: tigers, leopards, rhinoceroses, and deer. In the last 75 years, however, many of those animals have disappeared. People have cleared the forests to grow crops, and the animals' habitat has suffered.

Think

What part of the world is the article about? Look at the map.

Man-Eaters

Usually, it's humans who scare and kill animals, but it can be the other way around. About a hundred years ago, a few starving tigers and leopards terrified the people who lived in the foothills. Instead of eating other animals, like buffalo and antelopes, some of these big cats started killing and eating people! The cats had names like the Tiger of Chowgarh, the Thak Man-Eater, the Champawat Tigress, and the Panard Leopard.

Jim Corbett

Corbett, the Hunter

As a small boy, Jim Corbett was fascinated by wildlife. He taught himself to identify animals and birds by the sounds they made. Later, Jim became a tracker and hunter. The government asked him to track and shoot the man-eating tigers to protect people. Between 1907 and 1938, Corbett shot and killed nineteen tigers and fourteen leopards. He did this on foot, sometimes accompanied by his dog, and he took many risks to save people's lives. The first tiger he shot was the Champawat Tiger, a tiger that killed more than 436 people. Jim was a hero!

Corbett, the Naturalist

Jim wondered why the tigers and leopards were killing people. When he examined the cats that he had shot, he made an important discovery. They all had injuries. Some had gunshot wounds from poachers who hunted them illegally. Poaching was common because people could sell tiger skins for decoration and tiger bones for medicine. One tiger had a gunshot wound in its mouth, and its teeth were damaged. It could no longer attack buffalo and antelopes. Other tigers had injuries and infections from porcupine quills getting stuck in their skin. The reason they were eating people was that they couldn't hunt other animals.

Corbett National Park and Corbett's Tiger

After his discoveries, Jim became interested in conservation. He had a new mission: the preservation of tigers. He gave lectures and inspired people to respect wildlife—especially the big cats, which he loved and respected. Two years after he died in 1955, the oldest national park in India got a new name: Corbett National Park. It's a sanctuary for tigers, leopards, and other endangered animals. There's even a species of tiger named after Jim called Corbett's Tiger. No one is sure what the total population of Corbett's Tigers is, but there may only be 350 worldwide.

Think
What do you know about Jim Corbett?

Saving the Tiger

In the early twentieth century, there were about 40,000 tigers in India. Now there may be as few as 2,000. But thanks to conservationists like Jim Corbett, there are now more than 35 tiger reserves in India. Saving the tiger means preserving the entire food chain. First, we need to save the tigers' food, and that means protecting deer and other animals. Next, we need to save plants, trees, and grasses so that these animals can eat. By saving the plants, trees, and grasses, we protect our forests and rivers and all the birds, animals, and insects that live there. Very importantly, this means we are saving our water because, as you know, nothing on Earth can live without water.

Understand

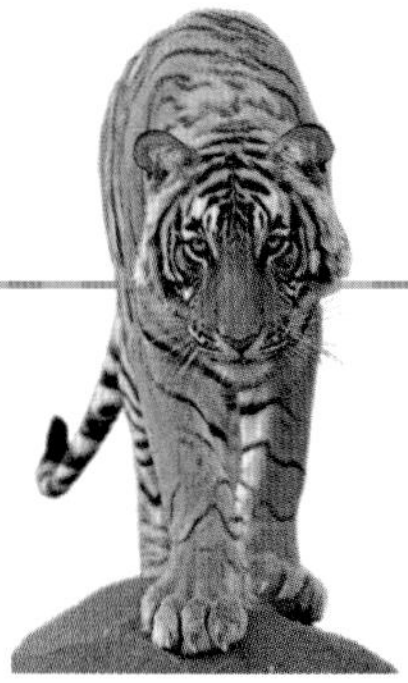

Comprehension

Think **Talk about "Save Our Tigers!" What did you learn that you didn't know before? Tell your partner about three things you learned from this article.**

A **Work in groups. Re-read the article and look at the pictures to help you answer the questions. As you read, monitor your understanding.**

1 Why are there fewer animals in the foothills today than there used to be?
2 Why did Jim Corbett change from a hunter into a conservationist?
3 Why is it important to save tigers?

B **Match the statements to the headings in the article. Look back at the article if you need to.**

1 Many different types of animals used to live in the hills.	a The Foothills of the Himalayas
2 The government wanted to protect people, so it hired a hunter.	b Man-Eaters
3 There are fewer tigers today than there were in the last century.	c Jim Corbett
4 People gave the man-eating tigers names.	d Saving the Tiger

C **Words in Context** **Look again at the words you circled in the article. Write them in the correct sentences.**

1 Corbett ____________________ is a sanctuary for tigers and other endangered animals.
2 ______________ are very hot and humid habitats.
3 Jim Corbett was a ______________ who became a conservationist.
4 The poor tiger died from its ______________.
5 Jim Corbett's ______________ was to protect tigers from poachers.
6 Sharks, rabbits, snakes, and birds are all types of ______________.

Workbook Grammar
pages 14–15

Grammar in Use

D Listen and read along. Then circle True (T) or False (F). 1•11

1 Lions live in natural habitats. T F

2 Sonya has a clean bedroom. T F

E **Learn Grammar** Review of Tenses

Simple Present	Tigers **go** to the river every day.
Present Continuous	Tigers **are going** to the river to drink.
Simple Past	Tigers **went** to the river yesterday.

Use the **Present Perfect** to:

- talk about things that have happened up to now.
  People have cleared forests to grow crops.
- say that something happened in the past but has an effect in the present.
  The animals' habitat has suffered.
- say that something started in the past but is still happening now.
  Tigers have always lived in thick jungles.

Identify and write the correct tense.

1 How long have you lived here? ______________________

2 My day is going well. ______________________

3 I went to the park last weekend. ______________________

4 I go to school every day. ______________________

F Talk with your partner. Make statements using the four tenses.

Communicate

Listening

Think Look at the picture. What do you know about this animal? What do you want to know?

A **Listen to the conversation. Circle True (T) or False (F).** 1•12

1	The giant panda is rare.	T	F
2	The giant panda isn't a member of the bear family.	T	F
3	There are about 16,000 wild pandas left.	T	F
4	A panda can weigh 150 kilograms.	T	F
5	Pandas spend 20 hours a day eating bamboo.	T	F
6	A panda can eat 37 kilos of bamboo in a day.	T	F
7	The bamboo pandas eat flowers every 30 to 80 years.	T	F
8	There are 100 panda reserves in China.	T	F

B **Listen again. Correct the false answers in exercise A. Then compare with a partner.** 1•13

Speaking 1•14

C **Think of possible answers to these questions. Give reasons using words like *I think it is* or *was because* and *it might be because.* Ask questions using *who, when, why, what, where,* and *how.***

Answer the questions.

- **Will tigers survive?**
- **How did Jim Corbett help tigers?**

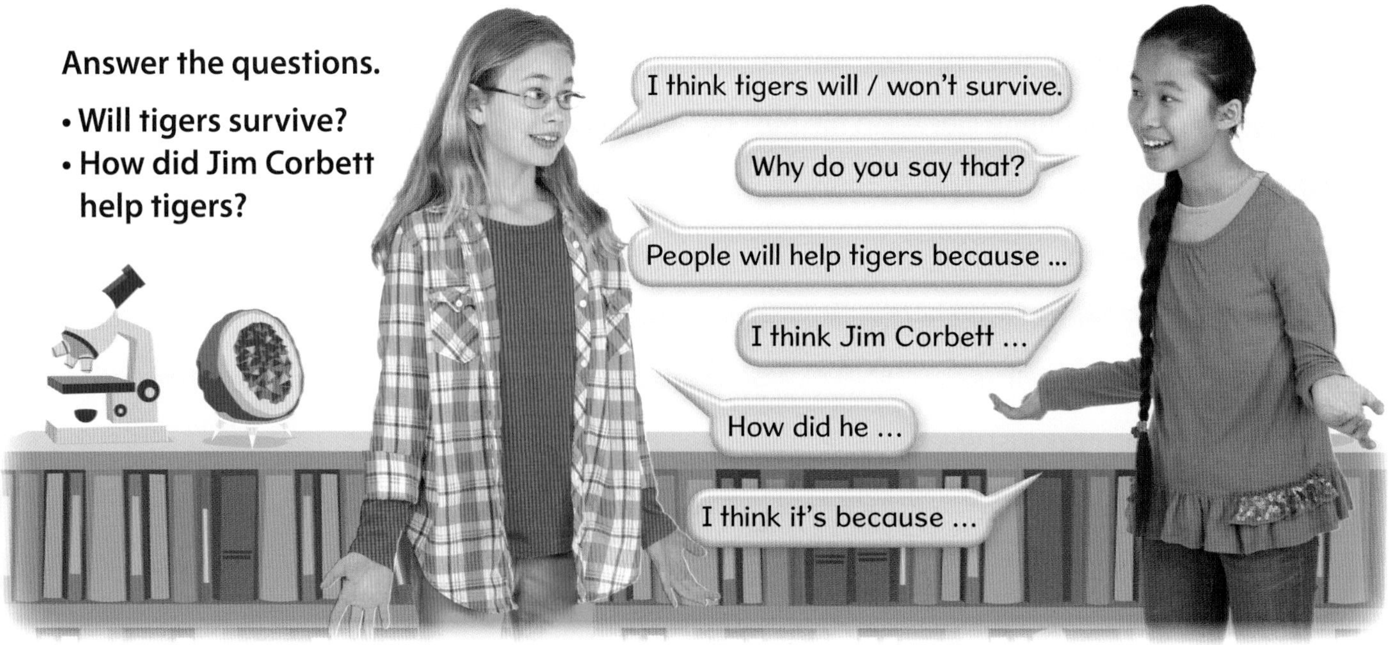

Word Study

D **Learn** Synonyms

Adjectives help you write in a more interesting way, but **synonyms** add variety to your vocabulary. Synonyms are words that mean almost the same thing.

Tigers are very fast.

You have to be quick to catch a rabbit.

Listen, say, and number the words. Then look them up in the dictionary. 1•15 A-Z page 192

____ starving ____ bright ____ timid ____ tale

____ error ____ preserve ____ provide ____ injure

E **Work with your partner. Take turns saying a synonym for each word in D.**

Writing Study

F **Learn** Irregular Past Verbs

Some verbs in the past are **irregular**. They don't follow the usual pattern.

Present	Past	
catch	caught	**She caught a cold.**
give	gave	**He gave me a gift.**

Complete each sentence with the correct verb form.

feel	hear	leave	sell	stand
felt	heard	left	sold	stood

1 Suddenly, I was all alone. When I saw the lion in the woods, I ______________ scared.

2 The animals were struggling. The zebras couldn't find any water, so they ______________.

3 Our class wants a tour. Does the animal sanctuary ______________ tickets for tours?

4 The buffalo began to run. The tracker ______________ up and walked toward the buffalo.

5 The animals in the jungle make lots of noise. I can ______________ the tigers roaring.

Write Now practice writing in the **Workbook**. page 17

Wrap Up

Writing

A **Read this persuasive e-mail.**

From: Nidia Romero

To: Amazon Bird Sanctuary

Subject: Please Save Golden Parakeets!

Salutation — Dear Bird Sanctuary,

Body —

I'm writing to you about golden parakeets. They belong in your bird sanctuary. They need your help because they're endangered. These beautiful birds live in the rainforests in northern Brazil. There are only about two thousand golden parakeets still alive!

Golden parakeets have become endangered because people have been destroying the rainforests. When rainforests disappear, the birds lose their homes. Since these parakeets are so beautiful, people also want them as pets. Many birds are captured and sold in pet markets.

I know that dodos and elephant birds became extinct. It would be terrible for golden parakeets to become extinct, too. If they lived in your sanctuary, they would have a better chance of surviving because their habitat would be safe and people couldn't have them as pets.

Closing — Best wishes,

Signature — Nidia

B **Answer the questions.**

1 How does the writer open and close the e-mail?
2 What statements does the writer make at the beginning of the first paragraph?
3 How does the writer organize the information in the e-mail?

C Learn Writing a Persuasive E-mail

- Start your e-mail with a salutation.
- Make a clear statement in your first paragraph.
- Organize the information so that the reader knows why you're writing. Give reasons for writing and explain what you want the reader to do.
- End your e-mail with a closing.

Write Now go to the **Workbook** to plan and write your own e-mail. page 19

D Present your e-mail to the class.

1 Tell the class who you decided to write to.
2 Tell why you chose this person.
3 Explain what it is you want to persuade this person to do.
4 Read your e-mail to the class.
5 Remember to read your e-mail with expression. Try to persuade your classmates.
6 Use gestures to help make your point.

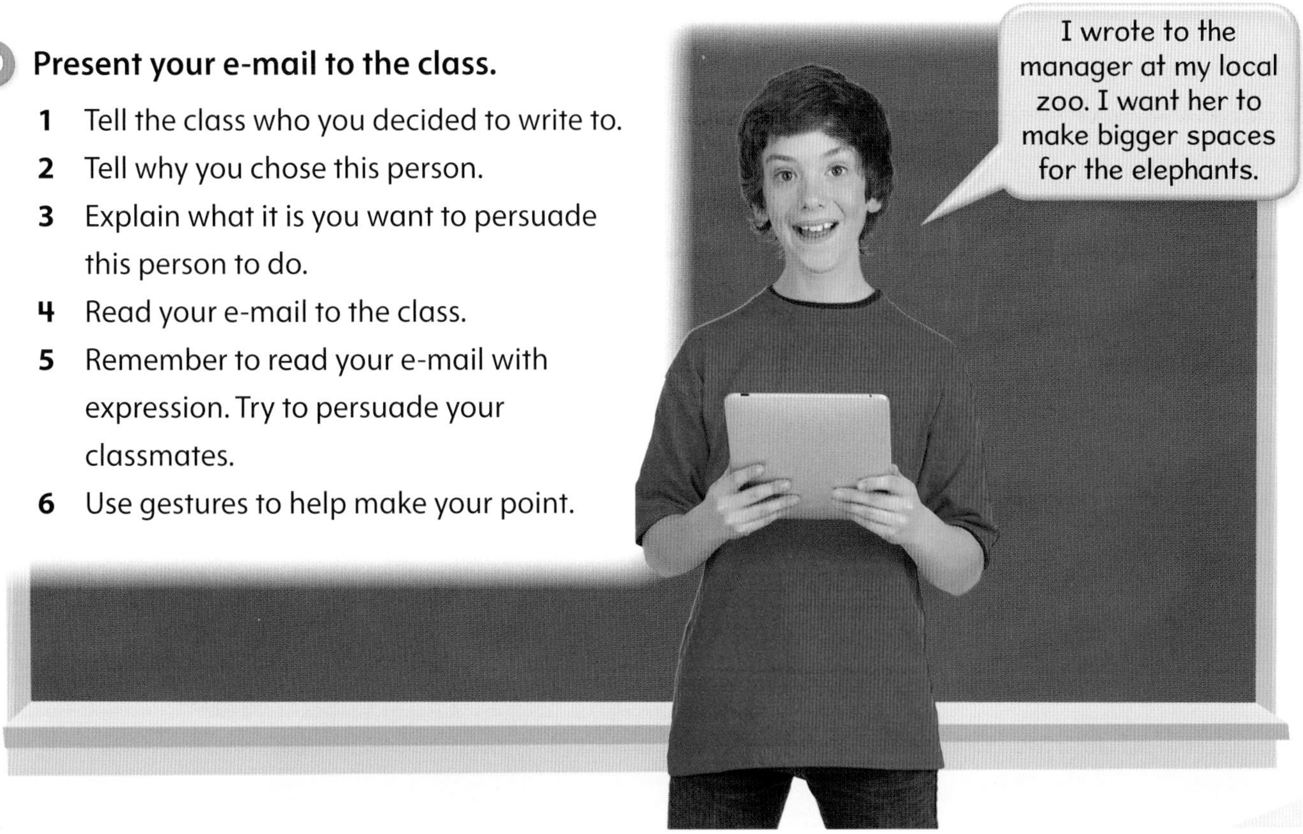

BIG QUESTION 1

Why do we protect animals?

A Watch the video. What endangered animals do you see?

B What are some answers to the Big Question? Talk about them with your partner.

C Complete the **Big Question Chart**. Then discuss it with the class.

In units **3** and **4** you will:

WATCH a video about teeth.

LEARN about how teeth are used for more than eating.

READ about teeth in humans and animals.

WRITE a report about teeth.

PRESENT your report to the class.

BIG QUESTION 2

What are teeth for?

A **Watch the video. Then talk about it with your partner.**

B **Look at the picture and discuss it with your class.**

1 What is the family doing?
2 How are they using their teeth?

C **Think and answer the questions.**

1 How many teeth do humans have?
2 What do you use your teeth for?
3 How do animals use their teeth?
4 What animals have sharp teeth?

D **Discuss this topic with your class. Fill out the Big Question Chart.**

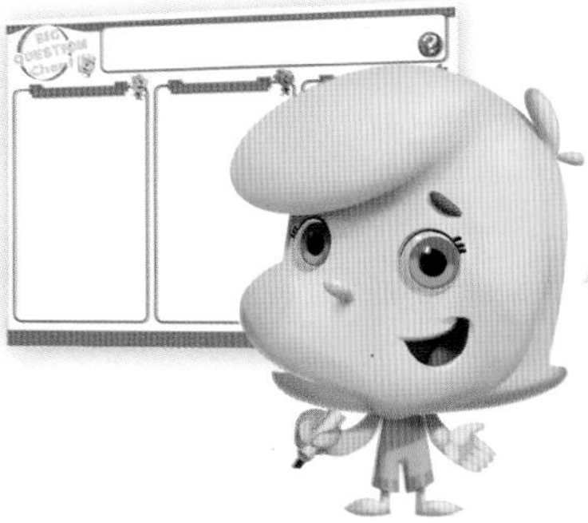

What do you know about teeth? What do you want to know?

UNIT 3 Get Ready

Words

A Listen and say the words. Then read and listen to the sentences. 1•16

incisor | canine | molar | carnivore | herbivore | omnivore

slice | grip | crush | cavity | gums | jaw

1 Humans have eight **incisor** teeth in their mouths.
2 **Canine** teeth are good for ripping food apart.
3 **Molars** are useful for grinding the food that we eat.
4 Lions, tigers, and leopards are all **carnivores**.
5 Cows, rabbits, and sheep are all **herbivores**.
6 Many people are **omnivores**. They eat meat, vegetables, and fruit.
7 Use that sharp knife to **slice** through the tomatoes.
8 You can **grip** things with your hands and your teeth.
9 Let's **crush** some ice for our sodas.
10 Ouch! I think I have a **cavity** in my tooth!
11 It's important to keep your **gums** and teeth healthy.
12 When the lion roared, I saw its huge **jaws** open wide.

B Look at the picture and number the words.

____ jaw
____ canine
____ incisor
____ molar
____ gums
____ cavity

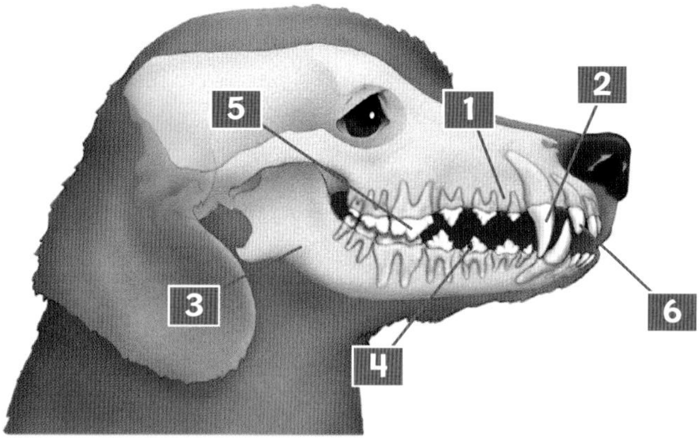

C Work with your partner to complete the sentences.

crush omnivores herbivores slice grip carnivores

1 ______________ eat meat.
2 ______________ eat plants.
3 It's hard to ______________ a snake.
4 ______________ the hard candy into small bits.
5 Knives are used to ______________ apples.
6 ______________ eat meat and vegetables.

Before You Read

Think **Answer the questions.**

1 When did you last go to the dentist?
2 Why did you go?
3 How did you feel?

D **Learn** Looking for Sensory Details

When you read, look for details that tell about the senses. Ask yourself what the character is seeing, smelling, hearing, feeling, or tasting.

Read the passage. What details do you notice about the five senses? Fill in the chart.

Mimo stepped into the dark garden. He could barely see a thing, but he felt a cold, sharp wind brush the side of his face. There was something strange in the night air. It smelled like a peach or maybe a mango. Mimo wondered if it was coming from the trees nearby, since he could hear a faint movement of leaves around him. All of a sudden, there was a cracking noise, like someone stepping on a dry tree branch. Mimo was scared. He pulled his jacket tight around him and walked on very quickly.

Hearing	Smell	Feeling	Sight
______	______	______	______
______	______	______	______
______	______	______	______

E **Words in Context** **Scan the poems on pages 30–31 and circle these words. As you read, try to guess what the words mean.**

detective **dental** **gravity** **filling** **treat** **munch**

F **Look at the poem on page 30 and read the first stanza. What do you think the poem is about?**

PREVIEW

"The Cavity" and "Have You Any Idea?"

In these poems, you'll read about a boy who goes to the dentist and three different types of animals. *Poetry* is written in lines or stanzas, not in paragraphs like a story. It often rhymes and has a rhythm. As you read, look for details that tell you what the characters are sensing.

Read 1·17

The Cavity

It started late one night.
I felt a nasty ache
Just after a big bite
Of yummy chocolate cake.

"It's dentist time for you,"
Dad told me the next day.
And since I couldn't chew,
I said, "I guess, OK."

My canines are bright white
Like tigers' teeth, I'd say.
I scrub them noon and night
And at the break of day!

My molars are all shiny.
I brush them hard and long!
Maybe the hole is tiny.
Maybe Dad is wrong.

I sat in the big chair.
My jaws were open wide.
I told the dentist where
I had a pain inside.

Is my tooth defective?
Dear dentist, please explain!
You are the great detective
Who cures all dental pain.

He said I had a cavity
Right inside my tooth.
He said so with such gravity
It had to be the truth!

"Is it in my incisor?"
I asked him with a smile.
I should have been much wiser
And kept quiet for a while.

"You'll need a little filling,"
The dentist softly said,
And then he started drilling
Right inside my head!

I heard a funny buzz,
Like an angry bee,
But I knew just what it was.
It didn't worry me!

And when the hole was filled,
I jumped down off the chair
For I was really thrilled
To get right out of there!

Think
How does the boy in the poem feel? Have you ever felt like that?

Have You Any Idea?

Have you any idea
What the carnivore saw
Scurrying through the trees?
A snack, a snack, a snack, a snack
That's tastier than cheese!

Have you any idea
What the carnivore did
When it saw its prey?
Attack, attack, attack, attack
Before the prey could stray!

"I have canine teeth, you see, dear prey,
And they will tear you up!"

Have you any idea
What the herbivore saw
Growing towards the sun?
A treat, a treat, a treat, a treat
Big and green and fun!

Think
What do the sensory details in this poem tell you?

Have you any idea
What the herbivore said
When it saw the grass?
"No meat, no meat, no meat, no meat
Just grass that is first class!"

"I have incisor teeth, you see, dear grass,
And they will nibble you down!"

Have you any idea
What the omnivore saw
Reaching up to the skies?
A lunch, a lunch, a lunch, a lunch
A mountain of tasty pies!

Have you any idea
What the omnivore said
When it saw all kinds of food?
"I'll munch, I'll munch, I'll munch, I'll munch
Because I'm in the mood!"

"I have molar teeth, you see, dear food,
And they will chew you to bits!"

Comprehension

Think Which poem did you like more? Tell a partner about three things you liked.

A What sensory details are in the poems? Fill in the chart.

Hearing	Feeling	Sight	Smell
______	______	______	______
______	______	______	______
______	______	______	______
______	______	______	______

B Answer the questions.

"The Cavity"

1 Which teeth does the boy talk about?

2 Does the boy brush his teeth regularly?

3 What does the dentist say the boy needs?

4 Is the boy happy at the end of the poem?

"Have You Any Idea?"

5 Who has to chase food?

omnivore herbivore carnivore

6 Who finds food growing?

herbivore omnivore carnivore

7 Who eats all types of food?

carnivore herbivore omnivore

C **Words in Context** Look again at the words you circled in the poems. Then use them to complete the sentences.

1 Police Captain Marcos was world famous for being a very clever ______________.

2 He ate a tasty ______________ at the party held at his police station.

3 Unfortunately, he woke up with terrible ______________ pain.

4 One of his molars was hurting so badly he couldn't ______________ on anything.

5 "The ______________ of this situation is clear," said the dentist.

6 "You have a large cavity, so you'll need a ______________."
Captain Marcos did not feel very clever that day!

Grammar in Use

D **Listen and read along. Then circle the correct answer.** 1•18

Did Finn ride a bike when he was nine? **Yes** **No**

E **Learn Grammar** Modals of Ability

Remember: Use **could** and **couldn't** to say that you did or didn't know how to do something in the past.

I could read by the time I was four.
I couldn't chew after I got a cavity.

The future of **can** / **can't** is **will** / **won't be able to**.

Next year, I will be able to ride my bike to school. I won't be able to drive a car.

Match the two halves of each sentence.

1 Next year, I'll • • a couldn't ride a bike.

2 We won't be • • b can speak Spanish and English.

3 Could you • • c able to go to the party tomorrow.

4 Last year, my sister • • d use a computer when you were four?

5 Right now, I • • e be able to join the baseball team.

F **Look at the times below. Talk with your partner about what you could or couldn't do in the past and what you will be able to do in the future.**

Past: ten years ago five years ago a year ago
Future: five years from now ten years from now

Communicate

Listening

Think Why is following instructions important?

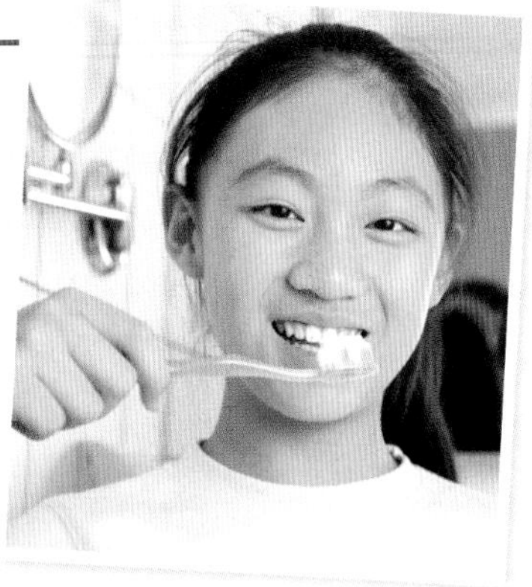

A **Learn** Listening for Instructions

When you listen, listen for instructions. Instructions are things people tell you to do, usually to help you do something better.

Listen. What kind of instructions is the woman giving? 1•19

B **Listen again. Then number the steps in the correct order.** 1•20

____ Brush the chewing surfaces of your teeth.

____ Squeeze out a pea-sized bit of toothpaste.

____ Brush the outside surfaces of your teeth.

____ Brush the inside surfaces of your teeth.

Speaking 1•21

C **Think about these questions. Then discuss them with a partner.**

- **Is it important to take care of your teeth?**
- **Why is it important to go to the dentist?**
- **What could happen if you don't take care of your teeth?**

Word Study

D **Learn** Prefix *in-*

Remember: A prefix is added to the beginning of a word. It changes the meaning of the word. The prefix in- means "not" and makes an opposite.

If your brushing is inadequate, you could get a cavity.

Listen and say the words. Write the opposites by adding *in-*. 1•22 A-Z

1 visible ____________ 3 accurate ____________

2 complete ____________ 4 credible ____________

E **Work with your partner. Write a sentence for each word above and its opposite.**

Writing Study

F **Learn** Adjective + Preposition

Some adjectives always have a preposition after them.

I'm interested in sports.

He's afraid of heights.

Are you good at math?

Write sentences about you.

1 I'm bad at ____________.

2 I'm excited about ____________.

3 I'm careful with ____________.

4 I'm interested in ____________.

Write Now practice writing in the **Workbook.** page 29

BIG QUESTION 2

What are teeth for?

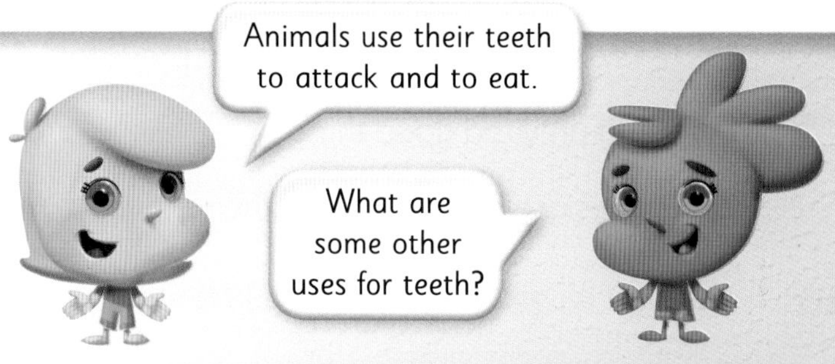

UNIT 4 Get Ready

Words

A Listen and say the words. Then read and listen to the sentences. 1•23

fang	tusk	venom	shelter	dam	prey
gnaw	pierce	fend off	wear down	lap up	create

1 The cobra has huge **fangs** in its mouth.
2 Both elephants and walruses have **tusks**.
3 Be careful! Many snakes carry **venom** in their fangs.
4 The hikers built a **shelter** in the woods.
5 A **dam** across a river stops water from flowing.
6 The lion caught its **prey**, an antelope.
7 A mouse **gnawed** through our telephone wire!
8 **Pierce** the potatoes before you bake them.
9 Some animals **fend off** predators by making noise.
10 By the end of the summer, my sneakers were **worn down**.
11 The cat **lapped up** the milk.
12 I like to **create** pictures and poems.

B Circle the one that doesn't belong.

1	tooth	fang	tusk	lip
2	home	yard	shelter	house
3	gnaw	nibble	chew	drink
4	attack	exhaust	tire	wear down

C Circle True (T) or False (F).

1 You can lap up water but not bread. T F
2 All animals carry venom. T F
3 You can create a song, a story, and a painting. T F
4 A dam allows water to flow quickly down the river. T F
5 *Fend off* means "to scare away a predator." T F
6 Being prey is a good thing. T F
7 Snakes use fangs to pierce their prey. T F

Before You Read

Think Answer the questions.

1 Do all animals have the same kinds of teeth?
2 What kinds of teeth do carnivores need?
3 What kind of teeth do snakes have?

D **Learn** Using Visuals

Visuals can help you understand the meaning of what you're reading, especially in nonfiction texts. When you read, remember to look at any pictures, graphics, diagrams, or other visuals. Think about how each visual relates to what you're reading. Be sure to read any captions, too.

Read the paragraph and look at the diagram. Talk with your classmates about how the visual helps you understand the text.

A Horse's Mouth

A horse has two sets of teeth in its lifetime, just like you do. It loses its baby teeth during the first few years of its life, and then it gets a permanent set. Unlike you, a horse has 40 teeth (you have 32). They have 24 premolars and molars to grind down food, 12 incisors for tearing grass, and 4 canines.

E **Words in Context** Scan the text on pages 38–39 and circle these words. As you read, try to guess what the words mean.

powerful intruders supply seal toppling lodge

F Look at the visuals on pages 38–39. What animals will you learn about in this text?

TEETH: Not Just for Eating

In this *informational text*, you'll discover what various animals use their teeth for. Informational texts include facts and are often used in schoolbooks, magazines, and on the Internet. As you read, use the visuals to understand the text.

Life Science

Author Amy Fernando wrote this science article for *Boys' Quest* magazine.

Read 1•24

Teeth: Not Just for Eating

By Amy Fernando

What are teeth used for? "That's easy," you say. "Teeth are for eating." You're partially right. For people, that's the purpose of teeth: biting off and chewing food (and occasionally ripping into that package of cookies). For animals, teeth are good for more than just eating. They might be used for fighting, communicating, or even building a home.

Some animals have a continuous supply of teeth. The shark has two sets of teeth, so a missing tooth is automatically replaced. Many reptiles like lizards also have a constant supply of new teeth replacing the old ones.

Many animals use their teeth to battle. Walruses have two ivory teeth called tusks that can grow up to almost a meter long. Male walruses fight each other over females, and the one with the longest tusks usually wins. Elephants also have tusks, though theirs can grow to be over three meters long! They use them to protect mates and young, even fending off lions if necessary.

Think

Look at the pictures to help you understand the text.

Other animals may attack prey with their teeth. Alligators and crocodiles don't use their teeth to chew, but to seize prey, which they swallow whole. They may lose teeth, but backups are waiting to move up and fill the empty spots.

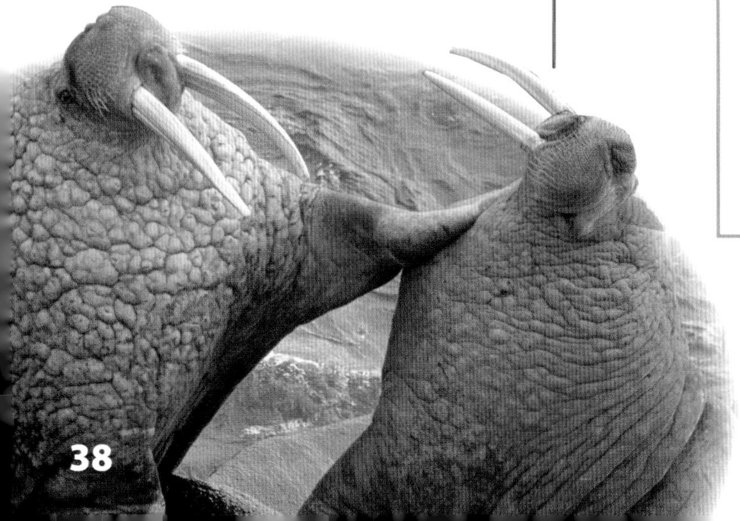

Some animals have sharp front teeth called fangs, which kill. A poisonous snake can push venom through its fangs, leaving its victim helpless. Vampire bats use fangs to pierce holes in their prey's fur and skin. Then they lap up the blood (their food) with their tongues. Hyenas' small teeth are set in powerful jaws that can crush the bones of a much larger animal.

Some animals use their teeth to send a message. Horses show teeth to express different feelings. They might talk tough, welcome others, or show respect. Porcupines click their teeth to warn others to stay away, while hippos yawn to threaten. Baboons scream and show a mouth full of huge, pointed teeth to both frighten intruders and make their young behave. Angry bison grind their teeth, making a squeaky sound. Stay away!

A few animals use their teeth to supply shelter. Naked mole rats use four razor-sharp teeth to dig tunnels, which serve as a home. (Their lips seal behind their teeth so that soil doesn't enter their mouths.) Their teeth are constantly growing, but wear down as the top and bottom teeth scrape together while digging through hard soil. Beavers also have four front teeth that continually grow. These teeth wear down from gnawing through trees. After toppling a tree, beavers use their teeth to drag logs to the water. They use these logs to build a home, or lodge, and also to create a dam, which protects the lodge.

Some animals also use their teeth to groom, or clean, themselves. For example, there is a group of animals called prosimians, which means "before the monkeys." They're monkey-like creatures, but they aren't monkeys. There are about 50 animals in this group, including lemurs, aye-ayes, and lorises. The type of teeth and the way they use them tell us that they must be prosimians. Almost all prosimians have comb-like lower front teeth that they use to clean the fur on their bodies.

Think

Have the pictures helped you understand the text?

So, as you can see, teeth are not only used for eating. They're also useful for building shelters, digging holes, warning off predators, catching and killing prey, fighting, and keeping clean!

Understand

Comprehension

Think Talk with your partner about three new things you learned about how animals use their teeth. Which animal's teeth do you think are the most interesting?

A Write three sentences describing the ways the visuals helped you to understand the text. Then compare your sentences with your partner's.

B Circle True (T) or False (F).

1 Sharks and lizards have teeth that replace themselves. T F

2 Walruses have fangs. T F

3 Alligators and crocodiles use their teeth to catch prey. T F

4 Some snakes have venom in their fangs to kill prey. T F

5 Horses use their teeth to kill other animals. T F

6 Beavers topple trees with their teeth. T F

C **Words in Context** Look again at the words you circled in the text. Then match the two halves of each sentence.

1 Unlike humans, some animals have a

2 In the storm, we saw a tree

3 My friends stayed at a

4 The notice said,

5 Hyenas have very

6 Please seal

a the bag before you put it away.

b continuous supply of teeth.

c "Intruders stay away!"

d powerful jaws that can crush bone.

e lodge in the mountains.

f topple over in the wind.

Workbook Grammar pages 34–35

Grammar in Use

D **Listen and read along. Then circle the correct answer.** 1•25

1 Charlie thinks it's a giraffe because it has **a long neck / spots.**

2 Sonya thinks it isn't an ostrich because it doesn't have **stripes / feathers.**

E **Learn Grammar** Modals of Certainty

Use **must** or **has to** to say you're sure that something is true.

It must be a prosimian. It has comb-like lower teeth.
It has to be a spider. It has eight legs.

Use **can't** to say you're sure that something isn't true.

That can't be a spider! It only has four legs.

Use **might** if you're not sure that something is true.

It might be a spider, but I'm not sure. I can't see how many legs it has.

Read the descriptions. Write what you think each animal must be.

1 It's big and gray with long tusks and a trunk.

____

2 It has long, poisonous fangs.

____

3 This type of animal uses its teeth for grooming.

____

4 This animal clicks its teeth as a warning.

____

F **Take turns describing an animal. Guess what animal it is. Use** ***might, has to, must,*** **and** ***can't.***

Communicate

Listening

Think What do you think this whale eats?

A **Listen to the conversation. Are killer whales carnivores or omnivores?** 1•26

B **Listen again and circle the correct answer. There may be more than one correct answer.** 1•27

1 Killer whales are _____

- **a** the biggest predators of warm-blooded animals.
- **b** the top predators in the ocean.
- **c** the biggest predators of cold-blooded animals.
- **d** the largest mammals on Earth.

2 Killer whales eat _____

- **a** seaweed.
- **b** fish.
- **c** seals, sea lions, and walruses.
- **d** fishing boats.

3 Killer whales hunt _____

- **a** alone.
- **b** in pairs.
- **c** in groups.
- **d** with other killer whales.

4 Killer whales have _____

- **a** small teeth.
- **b** large teeth.
- **c** over 40 teeth.
- **d** bad teeth.

Speaking 1•28

C **Learn** Comparing Things

Compare things using comparative adjectives + than.

I think killer whales are more dangerous than dolphins because dolphins don't hurt people.

Work with a partner. Think of animals you've learned about in this module and compare them.

- **Which is more dangerous?**
- **Which is more interesting?**

Word Study

D **Learn** Suffix *-ment*

The suffix -ment is sometimes added to a verb to make it a noun.

achieve + ment = achievement

I have no cavities! That's quite an achievement.

Listen and say the words. Write the words adding *-ment*. 1•29 A-Z

1 assess

____

2 treat

____

3 improve

____

4 agree

____

5 encourage

____

6 govern

____

7 measure

____

8 punish

____

E **Work with your partner. Use each verb in a sentence. Then use each noun you made by adding *-ment*.**

Writing Study

F **Learn** Parallel Structure with *-ing*

Use the same pattern of words to show that two or more ideas are equally important.

Wei enjoys playing, singing, and acting.

Write sentences about you.

1 I like __________, __________, and __________.

2 I sometimes go __________, __________, and __________.

3 I don't like __________ or __________.

4 In school, I like __________, __________, and __________.

5 __________, __________, and __________ are my favorite foods.

Write Now practice writing in the **Workbook**. page 37

Writing

A Read this report.

Title — **A Day in the Life of a Tiger's Teeth**

Introduction — The tiger is a carnivore from the cat family. It hunts other animals for food. The tiger only eats animals that it has caught by itself. It has a very wide mouth with big jaws and strong teeth. Besides catching prey with its teeth, it also carries its cubs (baby tigers) around in its mouth. It does that very gently so that the cubs don't get hurt.

Heading — **1. Canines**

The tiger has large canines. The tiger's upper canines are the largest of all the big cats, like lions and leopards. They're up to 6 centimeters in length, or the size of a man's finger! The tiger uses these sharp, pointed teeth to bite and kill its prey.

Illustration —

Caption — **A Tiger's Mouth**

2. Incisors

Incisors are strong enough to cut through tough skin. These are the smaller, sharp teeth that the tiger uses to seize its prey and to tear flesh from bones.

3. Molars

The molars are the teeth that grind up the food. They chop up the food to make it easier to swallow.

Unlike the lion, the tiger only hunts at night. During the day, it sleeps. Tigers need strong healthy teeth to catch and eat their prey.

B Answer the questions.

1 How does the writer start the report?

2 What visual does the writer use to help us understand the report?

3 How does the writer organize the information?

C Learn Writing a Report

- Include a good title to get people interested.
- Start your report by giving some background information about the topic.
- Use visuals (pictures or diagrams) to help show the information in your report.
- Organize your report into sections with headings so it's easier to understand.

Write Now go to the **Workbook** to plan and write your own report. page 39

D Present your report to the class.

1 Explain what your topic is and why you chose it.
2 Tell the class what you find most interesting about your topic.
3 Read your report to the class.
4 If you've included an illustration to go along with your report, show it to the class.

BIG QUESTION 2

What are teeth for?

A Watch the video. What kinds of teeth do you see?

B What are some answers to the Big Question? Talk about them with your partner.

C Complete the **Big Question Chart**. Then discuss it with the class.

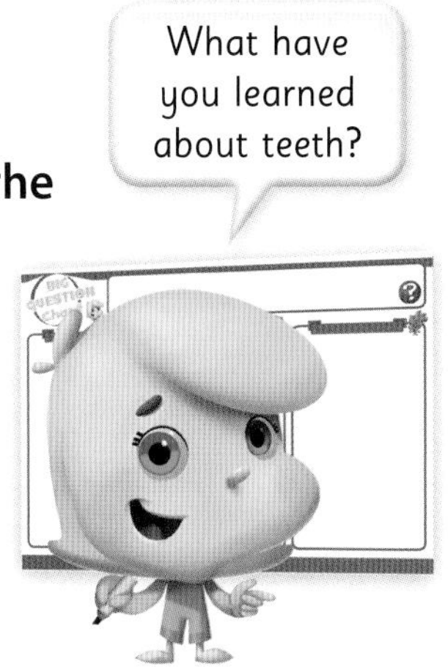

In units **5** and **6** you will:

WATCH a video about wheels.

LEARN about the many uses for wheels.

READ about wheels throughout history.

WRITE an opinion essay.

PRESENT your essay to the class.

BIG QUESTION 3

Why are wheels important?

A Watch the video. Then talk about it with your partner.

B Look at the picture and discuss it with your class.

1 What wheels do you see in the picture?
2 How would this picture be different if there were no wheels in our lives?

C Think and answer the questions.

1 What is a wheel?
2 What things have wheels?
3 What wheels do you use?
4 What wheels do people use just for fun?

D Discuss this topic with your class. Fill out the **Big Question Chart**.

UNIT 5 Get Ready

Words

A Listen and say the words. Then read and listen to the sentences. 1•30

transportation | transfer | haul | axle | rotate | spoke | rim | traction | gear | grind | technology | rod

1 Cars, trains, and planes are forms of **transportation**.
2 The bus broke down, so we **transferred** to another one.
3 People can **haul** goods with carts and horses.
4 Wheels on cars are connected by **axles**.
5 The Earth **rotates** around the sun.
6 The **spokes** on my bicycle wheels are made of thin metal.
7 The **rim** is the outer part of a wheel.
8 Our car lost **traction** when we drove on the ice.
9 **Gears** work with the chain on my bike to make it go.
10 You have to **grind** coffee beans before making coffee.
11 Computers and MP3 players are types of **technology**.
12 We used metal **rods** to hold up the tent.

B Look at the pictures and number the words.

____ axle
____ spoke
____ rim
____ rod
____ gear

C Write the words in the correct columns.

transportation haul traction technology grind rotate transfer

Verbs		Nouns	

Before You Read

Think Answer the questions.

1 How long ago do you think the wheel was invented?

2 Why do you think it was invented?

D **Learn** Re-reading

As you read, stop and think about what you just read. Did you understand it? If you did, keep reading. If you didn't, take your time. Go back and read it again.

Read the passage. Re-read anything you don't understand. Write notes in your notebook identifying the sections you re-read.

The London Eye

The London Eye is a giant Ferris wheel that was built in the year 2000. In 1993, a newspaper, *The London Times*, organized a competition to see who could design the best monument to celebrate the turn of the century. A company called Marks Barfield won the competition with its design for the London Eye. The company noticed that there weren't many places in London where people could see the skyline, and that's why they created this gigantic monument. Since it was built, over 20 million people have ridden on it and seen amazing views of the city.

Talk with your partner. What sections did you re-read? Use your notes.

E **Words in Context** Scan the text on pages 50–51 and circle these words. As you read, try to guess what the words mean.

platform **vehicle** **durable** **mill** **mechanical** **inspiring**

F **Look at the pictures on pages 50–51. What things with wheels do you recognize?**

PREVIEW

A Revolution in History

In this *informational text*, you'll learn how the wheel was invented and developed over time. Informational texts present facts about a subject. You can find them in books, magazines, and on the Internet. As you read, remember to re-read anything you don't understand.

Social Studies: History

Elizabeth Cody Kimmel is an award-winning author of over 30 books for children. She lives in a quiet, pretty town near New York City.

Read 1-31

A Revolution in History

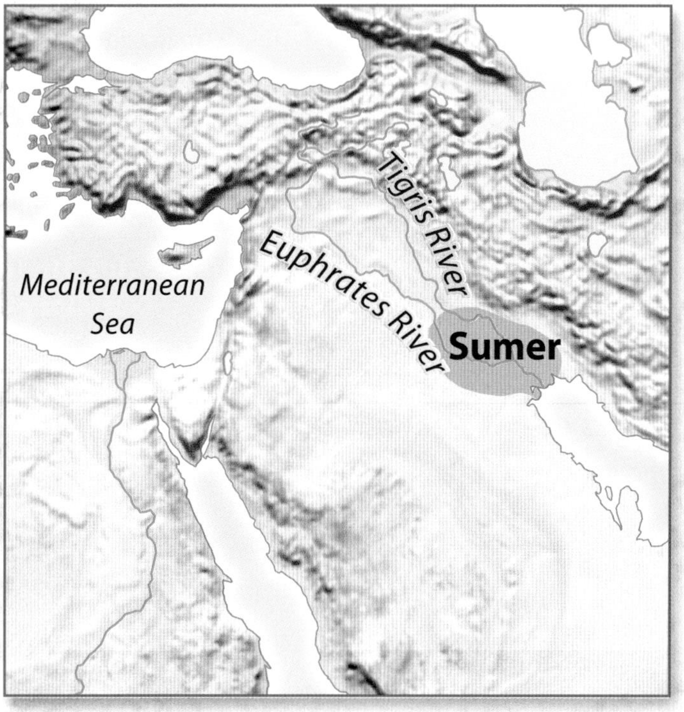

This region was one of the first to use wheels.

What would it be like if you had to go a whole day without using wheels? You'd have to walk everywhere, you wouldn't know what the time was, you'd have no books and no computers, and you'd have to carry everything you needed with you. It's a strange idea, isn't it?

We don't know who invented the wheel, nor do we know exactly when someone decided to use it for transportation, but we do know that the wheel completely changed the way people lived. It might just be the most important invention in our planet's history!

About five thousand years ago, before the wheel was invented, people relied on animals to transport many things. But if they wanted to haul really heavy things, like building stones, the animals weren't strong enough, so transportation was a big problem. Most things were moved using wooden rollers, like logs, but that was hard work.

Think

Do you understand everything? If not, re-read the paragraphs you're not sure about.

At least, it was hard work until a clever person from Sumer had a good idea. This person figured out that you could attach a wheel to both ends of a roller. That made an axle! And on top of the axle, you could put a wooden platform: a flat surface, like a sheet of wood. The axle kept the wheels in place, and the wheels rotated just the same way that rollers did. You could also get an ox or a donkey to pull it along, but even more importantly, you could carry a lot of things, and even people. Without realizing it, the Sumerian had invented the world's first vehicle.

In time, wheels became lighter and more durable.

Early wheels were made out of flat disks of wood, which were heavy and difficult to rotate. The Egyptians found a way to make a wheel that looked like a ring instead of a disk, making it much lighter. They attached support rods called spokes to the center of the wheel, and then they added an iron rim. All these improvements gave the wheel better traction and made it more durable.

The wheel didn't just change the way people got from place to place. Ancient man learned how to use the power of running water to turn large mill wheels. Small wheels called gears connected the mill wheel to a grinding machine. When the gears rotated, power was transferred from one to the other. This meant that people could make bread because they were able to grind wheat and make it into flour. The same idea of wheels and gears was used in the invention of a huge number of mechanical devices.

Machines of every size and shape, from watches and blenders to printing presses, wouldn't work if the rotation of wheel gears hadn't been developed. A day without wheels would mean empty schools and office buildings. Trucks and trains could not transport food to stores. Planes could not take off or land. There would be no bikes, skateboards, in-line skates, or robots. And even now, five thousand years after its invention, the wheel is still inspiring new technology. Wheels will always be a central part of life, and the need for them will grow as long as humans think, invent, and change.

Think

Do you understand everything? If not, re-read the paragraphs you're not sure about.

Today, we use wheels of all shapes and sizes. Wheels continue to make our lives easier.

Understand

Comprehension

Think Talk with your partner about three new things you learned from "A Revolution in History." What did you already know?

A Re-read the last paragraph on page 51. Answer the questions.

1 **Name two types of machines that wouldn't exist without the rotation of wheel gears.** ______________________
2 **What couldn't take off or land without wheels?** ______________________
3 **How do we transport food to stores?** ______________________

____

B Read the questions and discuss them in small groups. Compare your answers with the other groups.

1 When was the wheel invented?
2 Where was a wheel first attached to an axle?
3 What change did the Egyptians make to the wheel?
4 How were wheels used in a mill?
5 What is the most important use of wheels? Give your reasons.

C **Words in Context** Look again at the words you circled in the text. Then write them in the correct sentences.

1 Many people think the London Eye is an ______________ sight!
2 Metal is a very ______________ type of material.
3 A ______________ is used to transport things from one place to another.
4 The train stopped because of a ______________ problem.
5 You can grind pepper with a pepper ______________.
6 The principal stood on a ______________ and spoke to the whole school.

Workbook Grammar
pages 46–47

Grammar in Use

D Listen and read along. Then circle the correct answer. 1•32

Who do you think wins the race? **a** Finn **b** Charlie

E Learn Grammar **Future with *Will* and *Going to***

Use **will** to talk about facts in the future or to make predictions about things you believe will be true.

Future fact: **The sun will rise at 6:05 tomorrow.**

Prediction about belief: **Wheels will always be a central part of life.**

Use **going to** to talk about future plans or to make predictions about things you see.

Future plan: **I'm going to visit my uncle next week.**

Prediction about what you see: **Look at those big, black clouds. It's going to rain.**

Read the sentences. Write *prediction (seen)*, *prediction (belief)*, *future fact*, or *future plan*.

1 Vacation will begin on July 3rd and end on September 1st. ____________________

2 It's very windy. There's going to be a big storm tonight. ____________________

3 He's going to travel to Spain this summer. ____________________

4 Someone will find a cure for cancer someday. ____________________

F Choose a topic below and discuss it with your partner. Use *will* and *going to* to talk about the future.

vacation	university	weather
technology	jobs	age

I'll be 21 in ten years.

I'm going to be a doctor one day.

Communicate

Listening

Think What type of wheel do you think is the most important?

A **Listen to someone speak about the printing press. Then check (✓) the main idea.** 1•33

- [ ] Books used to be copied by hand.
- [ ] Rollers spread ink over paper.
- [ ] There would be no books and no education without wheels.
- [ ] The printing press gave us cheap books.
- [ ] The printing press is a machine that prints books.

B **Listen again. Then tell your partner two facts you heard while you were listening.** 1•34

Speaking 1•35

C **Plan two trips with your partner. Talk about where you are going and how you will get there.**

- school trip
- another country
- the beach

- car
- bicycle
- airplane
- train
- bus

Word Study

D **Learn** Compound Nouns

Make compound nouns by putting two nouns together.

skate + board = skateboard

Without wheels, there would be no skateboards.

Listen and say the words. Then match the words to make compound nouns. 1•36 A-Z

1 space	**2** wheel	**3** hand	**4** day	**5** ear	**6** door	**7** suit	**8** foot
a chair	**b** writing	**c** time	**d** ship	**e** print	**f** case	**g** bell	**h** ring

E **Work with your partner. Make a list of the compound words you matched above. Then find five other compound nouns to add to your list. Try words with *snow*, *sun*, *rain*, and *star*.**

Writing Study

F **Learn** Verb + Infinitive

Some verbs have an infinitive after them. An infinitive is a verb with to in front of it.

I agreed to go with him.
We decided to watch a movie.
He hopes to travel abroad one day.
He wanted to learn about history.

Complete the sentences with your own ideas. Use an infinitive after the verb.

1 I decided ______________________.

2 I promise ______________________.

3 I hope ______________________.

4 I plan ______________________.

Write Now practice writing in the **Workbook**. page 49

BIG QUESTION 3

Why are wheels important?

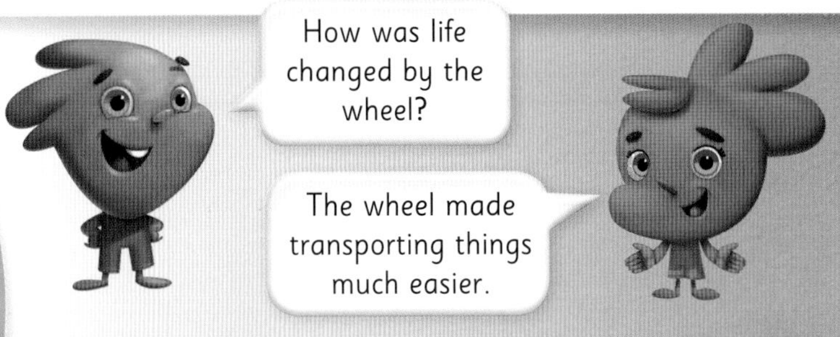

UNIT 6 Get Ready

Words

A Listen and say the words. Then read and listen to the sentences. 1•37

obedient | fortunate | tedious | exciting | fragile | determined
daring | foolish | thrilling | courageous | risky | fascinated

1 Kiko is **obedient**. He always listens to his parents.
2 I'm very **fortunate**. My family and friends are great.
3 This game is **tedious**! Let's play a less boring game.
4 Action movies are always **exciting**.
5 Do you think it's safe to cross the bridge? It looks **fragile**.
6 Joey was **determined** to pass the test, so he studied hard.
7 My brother is **daring**. He'll try anything!
8 Mom thinks I'm **foolish** for wearing T-shirts in the winter.
9 The roller coaster ride was **thrilling**!
10 You have to be **courageous** to be a firefighter.
11 It's too **risky** to cross the flooded river.
12 I was **fascinated** by the painting. I couldn't look away.

B Circle the correct word in each sentence.

1 If you want to succeed, you have to be **exciting / determined**.
2 Being lucky is very similar to being **fortunate / risky**.
3 Some dangerous activities, like skydiving, are also **thrilling / tedious**.
4 People who have risky jobs need to be **obedient / courageous**.
5 When crossing a street, children need to be **obedient / foolish**.
6 Mountain climbers must be **fragile / daring** to make it to the top.
7 Some scientists are **fascinated / determined** by life under the sea.

C Match. Then work with your partner to think of other answers to the questions.

1 What thing is risky? •	• **a** riding a bike without a helmet
2 What thing is exciting? •	• **b** fighting fires
3 What thing is tedious? •	• **c** a flower
4 What thing is daring? •	• **d** waiting a long time
5 What thing is fragile? •	• **e** graduating from school

Before You Read

Think How would your daily life be different without wheels?

D **Learn** Drawing Conclusions

Drawing conclusions helps you understand a story. To draw conclusions, think about these questions:

- What has happened so far?
- What do you know from your own life?
- What do you think will happen next?

Read the story and then fill in the chart.

Jeff and his family were driving from the city to go camping in the mountains. Jeff had never been to the mountains and couldn't wait to swim in the lake at the base of the hill. He wanted to dive right in!

For two hours, the car traveled on the steep mountain road. Finally, they arrived. First, they had to set up camp and have lunch. "Will I ever get to swim?" Jeff thought.

At last, Jeff jumped into his swimming gear and ran down the hill to the lake. He ran faster and faster toward the lake far below. "Oh, no," Jeff thought. "I've got to slow down!"

What has happened so far?	What do I know from my own life?	What will happen next?

E **Words in Context** Scan the story on pages 58–59 and circle these words. As you read, try to guess what the words mean.

settlement **longed for** **blurry** **figures** **propelling** **adjusted**

F Look at the pictures on page 58 and find the pogo stick. What's it for?

PREVIEW

Planet SinRota

In this *science fiction* story, you'll read about life on another planet. Science fiction is often about other worlds and different ways of life. Like other stories, a science fiction story has a plot, characters, and a setting. Draw conclusions about the story as you read.

Read 1•38

Planet SinRota

"Zoog, hurry!" yelled Zoog's dad. "Your grandmother is sick. She has a fever and purple spots. Take your pogo stick and fetch Doctor P721."

The obedient Zoog bounced off to the doctor's house as fast as his pogo stick would carry him. The doctor and his four assistants came and carried Zoog's grandmother away on a special bed to make her better. Fortunately, people always got better on planet SinRota, where illness rarely lasted more than 15 hours.

Zoog was tired. Earlier, he'd taken his pogo stick and hopped to school and back, a distance of 5.36 kilometers each way. He went up to his bedroom and looked through the brand-new telescope he'd received for his birthday the previous week. Zoog's life was tedious. His planet had no books, no clocks, no computers, and no TV. Far away in another settlement, Zoog had cousins, but there was no mail, so he couldn't communicate with them. Although he longed for a more exciting life, he felt fortunate that he had good friends and no serious problems.

Think
Why do you think there are no books, clocks, computers, or TVs on SinRota?

It was dark 17.7 hours a day on SinRota. Zoog searched the night sky, looking for the magical planet he'd seen many nights in a row. Suddenly, there it was! The blue planet! Zoog gazed at it. The picture was blurry, but he could see areas of water, distant mountains, and patches of bright light. "Who lives there," he wondered, "and what do they do?" If he looked hard at one spot for a long time, he occasionally glimpsed small figures with strange circular objects propelling them along.

Not only did Zoog have to go to school on a pogo stick, but it was also his job to do the shopping for his parents every evening. This meant dragging a heavy sled behind him to and from the store. At the store, he stacked up delicious orange munchballs and green yumsters

SinRotan Language **animoog:** a SinRotan animal, **munchball:** a SinRotan fruit, **yumster:** a SinRotan vegetable on the sled and pulled it home before darkness fell. Everything he bought was grown in his settlement because it was too risky to bring food from other parts of Planet SinRota. Nobody could drag sleds further than a few kilometers, and the food would be spoiled long before it could reach another settlement. Even the animoogs couldn't drag sleds very far, so it was foolish to attempt long journeys. Zoog had never left the area he lived in, 5.36 kilometers was his limit, but he dreamed of exploring further.

Zoog looked through his telescope again. He adjusted it slightly, and he was fascinated to see activity on the blue planet. The blurry figures he'd seen before suddenly came into sharp focus! There were figures driving around in vehicles of all shapes, sizes, and colors. There were figures riding bicycles. There were huge airplanes zooming fast up runways and flying into the air. It was thrilling! He also saw figures sitting on buses and trains, moving fast from one city to another. In a park, he could see small figures, children, playing on skateboards and in-line skates. They were leaping through the air. It looked incredibly daring. It was then that he had his big idea.

Think
Why does Zoog use a sled to bring the groceries home?

"I know what I'm going to do!" said Zoog. He began to draw pictures of everything he could see, these wonderful machines with circles that made them move! Trains, planes, bicycles, skateboards, cars, buses, wheelchairs, ambulances, taxis, carts, wheelbarrows, motorcycles, trucks, roller coasters, Ferris wheels, helicopters, strollers, windmills … Zoog drew all night long.

In the morning, Zoog ran downstairs and showed his parents the pictures. And in just a few short days, the history of SinRota changed completely and forever.

Thanks to Zoog and his telescope, planet SinRota now has wheels! Things will never be the same again.

Understand

Comprehension

Think Write down two things you found interesting about "Planet SinRota" and talk about them with your partner.

A What conclusions did you draw about "Planet SinRota"? Work with your partner to fill in the chart.

What has happened so far?	What do I know from my own life?	What will happen next?

B Circle the correct answer.

1 Zoog goes to school ____
- **a** by bus.
- **b** on his bike.
- **c** on a pogo stick.
- **d** in his dad's car.

2 SinRota's history changes because ____
- **a** Zoog draws pictures of people.
- **b** Zoog has a pogo stick.
- **c** Zoog sees oceans.
- **d** Zoog sees wheels.

3 On the blue planet, Zoog can see ____
- **a** figures.
- **b** animals.
- **c** munchballs.
- **d** rivers.

4 The blue planet is ____
- **a** Mars.
- **b** Earth.
- **c** Venus.
- **d** Jupiter.

C **Words in Context** Look again at the words you circled in the story. Match each word to its definition.

1 longed for •
2 figures •
3 blurry •
4 settlement •
5 adjusted •
6 propelling •

• **a** not sharply in focus
• **b** wished for strongly
• **c** moving something forward
• **d** changed something slightly
• **e** a place where people live
• **f** shapes of bodies

Grammar in Use

D **Listen and read along. Then circle the correct answer.** 1•39

Sonya and April are talking about the **present / future.**

E **Learn Grammar** Future with Present Continuous

You can use the **present continuous** to talk about future arrangements, especially when you mention a specific time or place.

Arrangement: **We are meeting our friends at 2:00 on Friday.**

Remember: Use **will** for future facts and predictions about things you believe will be true. Use **going to** for future plans and predictions about things you see.

Future fact: **The moon will rise at ten o'clock tonight.**

Prediction about belief: **Things will never be the same again.**

Future plan: **I'm going to take a music class next year.**

Prediction about what you see: **Look at those clouds. We're going to get wet.**

Circle the best choice for each sentence.

1 Arrangement: Tomorrow at ten, we **are meeting / will meet** our friends in the park.
2 Fact: On December 20th, I **am being / will be** twelve.
3 Prediction (belief): Someday, the whole world **will / is going to** use solar power.
4 Plan: They **are going to / will** hike in the mountains.
5 Prediction (seen): Look! There are big, gray clouds. It **will / is going to** snow.

F **Take turns asking and answering the questions with the present continuous, *will,* and *going to*.**

1 What are you doing after school?
2 How old will you be in five years?
3 What are you going to do this weekend?

Communicate

Listening

Think What do animals use wheels for?

A **Listen to the conversation. Circle the correct answer.** 1•40

1 The object is made of ____
   a wood.
   b metal.
   c plastic.

2 The object is ____
   a small and light.
   b big and heavy.
   c wide and long.

3 The object ____
   a is blue.
   b is noisy.
   c can be many colors.

4 The object is used by ____
   a people.
   b animals.
   c teachers.

B **Listen again. Write a sentence that tells what the object is used for.** 1•41

____

Speaking 1•42

C **Learn** Giving Advice

When you give advice, use **should** and **why don't you?**

You should ride a bike. It's good for your health.

Why don't you borrow my skateboard? I'm not using it.

Work with your partner. Choose a problem from the list and take turns offering advice.

- You missed the bus.
- Your bicycle has a flat tire.
- You want new skates.

Word Study

D **Learn** Prefix *mis-*

Remember: A prefix is added to the beginning of a word. It changes the meaning of the word. The prefix mis- means "bad" or "wrong."

mis + **behave** = **misbehave**

Zoog was a good boy. He didn't misbehave.

Listen and say the words. Write the words by adding *mis-*. 1•43 A-Z

1 treat ____________

2 trust ____________

3 communicate ____________

4 direct ____________

5 read ____________

6 remember ____________

7 calculate ____________

8 judge ____________

E **Work with your partner. Write sentences with each word above and the word you made by adding the prefix *mis-*.**

Writing Study

F **Learn** More Irregular Verbs

Remember: Some verbs are irregular when they are in the past tense.

become	→	became	**feel**	→	felt	**light**	→	lit
dig	→	dug	**draw**	→	drew	**give**	→	gave

Zoog drew all night long.

Write the correct form of the verb in parentheses.

1 I ____________ (draw) a picture of a car for our project last week.

2 The weather ____________ (become) rainy last night.

3 Sam ____________ (feel) very happy yesterday.

4 Yesterday, I ____________ (dig) holes in the garden for seeds.

5 The waiter ____________ (light) the candle at our table.

Write Now practice writing in the **Workbook**. page 57

Wrap Up

Writing

A Read this opinion essay.

Cars of the Future

Opening statement and opinion

In my opinion, the car of the future will be very exciting. I think that by 2020 we'll have cars that don't have a steering wheel. Instead, the car will have a computer on-board and it'll drive itself. People will be passengers instead of drivers. The software in the computer will guide the car along the road and even help it to park. Cars will be much safer because drivers make mistakes, but computers usually don't.

Second paragraph

These cars will be bigger than the cars we have today. In fact, they'll be more like buses than cars. This will be good for us, because the cars will be able to carry a lot of passengers. That's a good thing, because we won't need to use so much gas and we won't have as much pollution. If we don't have as much pollution, Earth will be a better place to live!

Conclusion

Finally, I think the new cars will have special TV screens inside them so people can work or play while they're riding to their offices or to school. That will save time for people who work in offices because they'll be able to read e-mails while they're going to work. And it will be fun for kids because they'll be able to watch programs or do their homework. The car of the future will be great!

B Answer the questions.

1 How does the writer start the opinion essay?
2 Whose opinion is the writer giving?
3 How does the writer organize the essay?

C Learn Writing an Opinion Essay

- Start an opinion essay with a statement that clearly gives your opinion.
- Use **in my opinion**, **I think that**, or **I believe that** to write about your opinion.
- Organize your essay into paragraphs and give information that explains your opinion.
- In your conclusion, write a final sentence that restates your opinion.

Write Now go to the **Workbook** to plan and write your own opinion essay. page 59

D Present your opinion essay to the class.

1 Tell the class what you're going to talk about.
2 Tell the class why you chose to write about this topic.
3 Read your essay to the class.
4 As you read, remember to smile and try to look up from your paper from time to time.
5 Stress the most important parts of your essay by choosing two or three places to use gestures.

BIG QUESTION 3

Why are wheels important?

A Watch the video. What kinds of wheels do you see?

B What are some answers to the Big Question? Talk about them with your partner.

C Complete the **Big Question Chart**. Then discuss it with the class.

Testing Practice 1

Reading and Writing

A **Read Anna's letter. Circle the best word (a, b, or c) to complete each sentence.**

> **Tip**
> Try all three choices before you mark your answer.

Dear Lucia,

Last Saturday, I visited my brother Carlos, the horse trainer. He teaches young horses to be (1) __________. It's a (2) __________ job because young horses can be wild. Carlos gets thrown off a lot, but he gets back on the horse right away. He is very (3) __________. He isn't scared at all. I think Carlos is lucky to have such an (4) __________ job.

Yours,
Anna

1	**a** inspiring	**b** obedient	**c** fortunate
2	**a** durable	**b** blurry	**c** risky
3	**a** courageous	**b** extinct	**c** rare
4	**a** durable	**b** exciting	**c** foolish

B **Read this e-mail from your friend Matt.**

From: Matt

Date: January 4

Hi! What are you going to do this weekend? I'm going to a national park. It's a sanctuary for bald eagles. Bald eagles were endangered until 2007. They are protected now. Do you like birds? What's your favorite animal?

Write an e-mail to Matt. Answer his questions in your notebook. Write 25–30 words.

Listening

C **You will hear two short conversations. You will hear each conversation twice. There are two questions for each conversation. Put a check (✓) by each right answer.** 1•44

> **Tip**
> Don't mark your answer until you have heard each conversation twice.

1 Where do some sharks live?

a 

b 

c 

2 What do sharks eat?

a 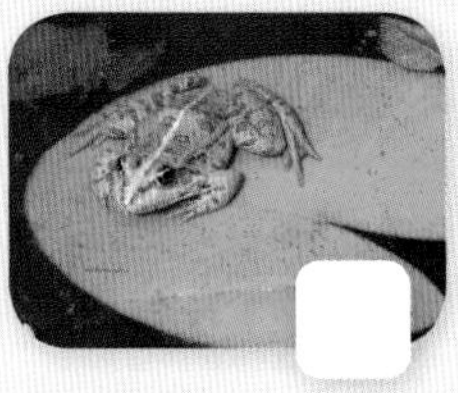

b 

c 

Now listen to the second conversation. 1•45

3 What do the boys see?

a 

b 

c 

4 What happens to the man?

a 

b 

c 

Speaking

> **Tip**
> Speak in a loud, clear voice.

Part 1 **Work with a partner. Ask and answer questions about school.**

1 What school do you go to?

2 What grade are you in?

3 What's your favorite subject?

4 Why is it your favorite subject?

Part 2 **Your teacher will give you a sheet of paper with some information on it. One of you will get questions and one of you will get answers. Ask and answer with your partner.**

Questions

Answers

In units **7** and **8** you will:

WATCH a video about communication.

LEARN how animals communicate.

READ about animal communication and a helpful dolphin.

WRITE
a descriptive essay.

PRESENT
your essay to the class.

BIG QUESTION 4

How do animals communicate?

A **Watch the video. Then talk about it with your partner.**

B **Look at the picture and discuss it with your class.**

1. What is the penguin doing?
2. What do you think it's trying to communicate?

C **Think and answer the questions.**

1. How do you communicate?
2. Why do you communicate?
3. How do you think animals communicate?
4. Can you think of some examples of animals that communicate?

D **Discuss this topic with your class. Fill out the Big Question Chart.**

UNIT 7 Get Ready

Words

A Listen and say the words. Then read and listen to the sentences. 2•02

race	drift	glide	wade	paddle	dive
splash	propel	float	sprint	jog	plod

1 He **raced** to the park to play with his friends.
2 The clouds **drift** slowly across the sky.
3 The fish **glides** smoothly through the water.
4 The boy **waded** into the shallow water in the lake.
5 She **paddled** her rowboat down the river.
6 My sister can **dive** into the deep water, but I can't.
7 The kids **splashed** water on each other.
8 The whale uses its tail to **propel** itself through the water.
9 He **floated** on his back in the pool.
10 She **sprinted** to the finish line.
11 For exercise, Jen **jogs** every morning in the park.
12 The old horse **plodded** slowly down the road.

B Write the words in the correct columns. Use some words more than once.

wade race paddle jog float sprint drift splash dive

On a Path	In the Air	In the Water

C Choose the best word to complete each sentence.

glides
plodded
propel

1 The tired runner ________________ toward the finish line.
2 She used a pair of oars to ________________ the boat forward.
3 The ice skater ________________ over the frozen lake.

Before You Read

Think What do you know about oceans? What stories have you read about oceans?

D **Learn** Character

When you read a story, pay attention to:

- the character's name
- what he or she looks like
- how he or she feels
- what the character says and does

You can use a character web like the one below to help you understand a character better.

Read the story and fill in the character web.

Marta brushed her long brown hair. She tried to smile as she glanced at herself in the mirror, but she knew it wasn't going to work. She was not looking forward to another day at school. Marta was a good student and her parents were very proud, so why was it so difficult to go to school? Marta was shy. Now it was worse, because she was in a new school with new people. Some days, she even tried to convince her father that she was too ill to go to school. "Everyone looks at me like I don't belong," she would tell her father.

How she feels: ____________________

Character's name: ____________________

What she says or does: ____________________

What she looks like: ____________________

E **Words in Context** Scan the story on pages 72–73 and circle these words. As you read, try to guess what the words mean.

fishing rod **chuckled** **hook** **beamed** **paddles** **grinning**

F **Answer the questions before you read.**

1 What is a storm?
2 How can a storm affect us?

PREVIEW

Magdi and the Dolphin

In this *narrative fiction* story, a friendly dolphin saves a boy named Magdi during a storm. Narrative fiction narrates or tells a story. It has characters, a plot, and a setting.
As you read, think about Magdi's character and how it can help you understand the story.

Read 2•03

Magdi and the Dolphin

Magdi looked out of the window and saw clear blue skies. "Yes!" he shouted. "It's a beautiful day! I can go fishing."

"Hi, Dad! Bye, Dad! It's a beautiful day! See you later!" shouted Magdi. He was so excited that he was speaking very, very fast. He rushed out of the house with his fishing rod.

"What did he say?" asked his sister.

"He said that it was a beautiful day for fishing," chuckled Magdi's dad with a big smile on his face. "He's always happy when he goes fishing."

Magdi raced to the beach and untied his little red fishing boat. *Maybe today I'll catch a fish for dinner!* he thought. He waded out into the warm blue water, pushing the boat until it floated. Then he jumped into it and paddled toward some rocks.

Magdi looked over the side of the boat and saw a lion fish. He knew that lion fish were very dangerous; they could sting you. Magdi sat and watched quietly as it dove under the boat and disappeared under a rock. Next, he saw a parrot fish, with its shiny blue, purple, and green scales, gliding through the water. *Parrot fish are tasty,* he thought. *Maybe today I'll catch a parrot fish.*

Magdi put a piece of bread on the hook of his fishing rod and threw the fishing line into the water. Then he threw more bread into the water to attract the fish. Suddenly, hundreds of fish swam up to the boat. There were bright yellow fish, black-and-white fish that looked like zebras, fish with long noses, and big, fat puffer fish. Magdi knew all their names. He beamed with delight. *Maybe I won't catch any fish today,* he thought. *They're beautiful! Maybe today I'll just watch them.* Magdi pulled his paddles into the boat, turned onto his stomach to watch the fish, and fell asleep in the warm sun.

Magdi woke up feeling chilly. Looking up,

Think
Who is the main character?
How does he feel?

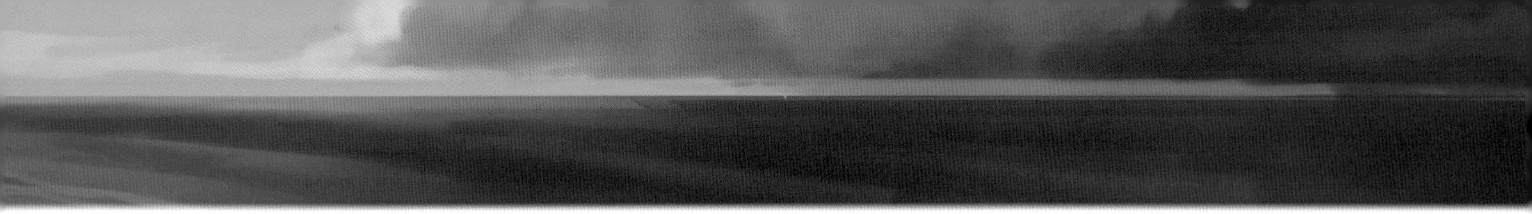

he saw black skies. Big waves were shaking his little red fishing boat, and it was drifting out to sea.

Two of Magdi's friends, Malik and Ali, were playing on the beach. "Hey, Magdi! Magdi!" they shouted. "Come back! There's a storm!" Their words floated across the water, carried by the wind.

"What did you say?" Magdi yelled.

"We said that there was a storm!" shouted Malik and Ali. "Come back!"

Uh-oh! thought Magdi. He tried to paddle towards the beach, but the waves pushed him further away. A huge wave crashed onto his boat, throwing him into the water.

"Oh, no! Help! Help!" Magdi cried. But just at that moment, he felt something under the water.

A *very big* something! Then, to his surprise, he was moving through the waves at high speed, heading straight for the beach. He looked down and saw a beautiful grinning face. It was a dolphin! The dolphin splashed and jumped through the water, carrying Magdi on its back. The dolphin used its powerful tail to propel its body through the water.

When they got to the shallow water, the dolphin dropped Magdi on the sand and then swam up and down in front of him.

"Thank you, my friend," whispered Magdi.

Every day afterward, Magdi and the dolphin played in the ocean. The dolphin taught Magdi tricks, such as how to dive deep down to the ocean floor, how to float, how to glide through the water, and how to stay away from a storm!

Think

How do you think Magdi feels when he sees the dolphin?

Understand

Comprehension

Think Talk with your partner about two or three things you liked about "Magdi and the Dolphin."

A Complete the character web with information about Magdi. Then discuss it with your partner.

Character's name: ____________

What he looks like:

How he feels:

What he says and does:

B Answer the questions.

1 Why did Magdi decide to go fishing?
2 Why was Magdi chilly when he woke up in the boat?
3 Why did Magdi whisper "thank you" to the dolphin?
4 What did you learn about Magdi?
5 How do Magdi and the dolphin communicate with each other?

C **Words in Context** Look again at the words you circled in the story. Write them in the correct sentences.

1 To catch fish, you need a ____________.
2 To propel a canoe, you have to learn how to use ____________.
3 I ____________ when I heard my friend's joke.
4 You must be very happy. You're ____________.
5 The girl ____________ a big smile when she saw her quiz results.
6 Put some bread on the ____________ and throw it into the water.

Grammar in Use

D **Listen and read along. Then check (✓) the correct answer.** 2•04

1	Who says that he's going fishing?	Finn ☐	Charlie ☐
2	Who tells Mom?	Finn ☐	Charlie ☐

E **Learn Grammar** Reported Speech with *Said That*

Reported speech tells what someone said by using the words **said that**. If the direct speech is in the present tense, the reported speech changes to the past tense.

Direct Speech	Reported Speech
"It's a beautiful day," said Magdi.	**Magdi said that it was a beautiful day.**
"I'm working," said Tom.	**Tom said that he was working.**

Work in groups of three to practice reported speech.

Step 1:

Student A, think about an animal you like. Whisper it to **Student B**.

Student B, think about an animal you don't like. Whisper it to **Student C**.

Student C, think about a bird you like. Whisper it to **Student A**.

Step 2:

Use reported speech.

Student A, tell your friends what bird **Student C** likes.

Student B, tell your friends what animal **Student A** likes.

Student C, tell your friends what animal **Student B** doesn't like.

Communicate

Listening

Think What kind of sound do you think a whale makes?

A **Listen and circle the words you hear. Compare your answers with a partner.** 2•05

fifteen   an hour   Atlantic Ocean   50 years   eighteen   eight

B **Listen again. Circle True (T) or False (F).** 2•06

1	Humpback whales live in oceans all over the world.	T	F
2	Scientists discovered the humpback whale's song about 50 years ago.	T	F
3	A humpback whale's song is between 50 minutes and an hour long.	T	F
4	Humpback whales in different oceans sing different songs.	T	F
5	Male and female humpback whales sing.	T	F
6	A humpback whale's song can travel thousands of kilometers.	T	F

Speaking 2•07

C **Learn** Asking for Clarification

When you're listening and speaking, you can ask someone to explain things. Use questions such as **What do you mean? Can you explain that? What happened?** and **How did that happen?** to ask for more information.

Think about something that happened to you. Take turns telling stories and asking for clarification.

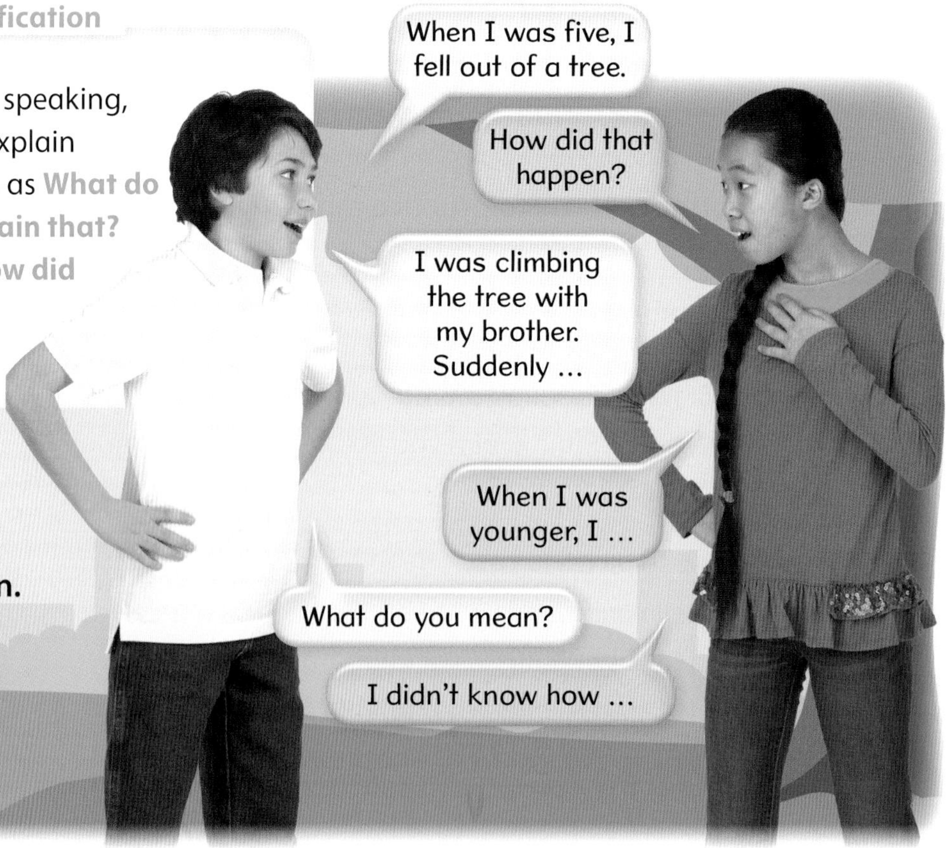

Word Study

D **Learn** Letter Combination *gh*

Some words have a silent **gh**, as in **caught** and **right**. Sometimes **-gh** has the sound of **f**, as in **laugh** and **tough**.

The dolphin glided through the water.
Rough waves tossed Magdi's boat.

Listen and say these words. Underline the silent *gh* sounds. 2•08 A-Z

1 cough	**2** tough	**3** though	**4** through
5 fought	**6** rough	**7** enough	**8** high

E **Work with your partner. Make lists of the words with silent *gh* and *gh* with the *f* sound. Then try to find three more words to add to each list.**

Writing Study

F **Learn** Commas and Semicolons

There are two ways to join two independent clauses:

1 Use a comma (,) and a conjunction (**and**, **or**, **but**, **for**, **yet**).
We had a big storm last night, but it cleared up this morning.
independent clause 1 — conjunction — independent clause 2

2 Use a semicolon (;) and no conjunction.
We had a big storm last night; it cleared up this morning.
independent clause 1 — semicolon — independent clause 2

Rewrite these sentences in your notebook by joining them in two different ways.

Humpback whales in the Pacific Ocean sing one kind of song.

Humpback whales in the Atlantic Ocean sing another kind of song.

Write Now practice writing in the **Workbook**. page 69

BIG QUESTION 4

How do animals communicate?

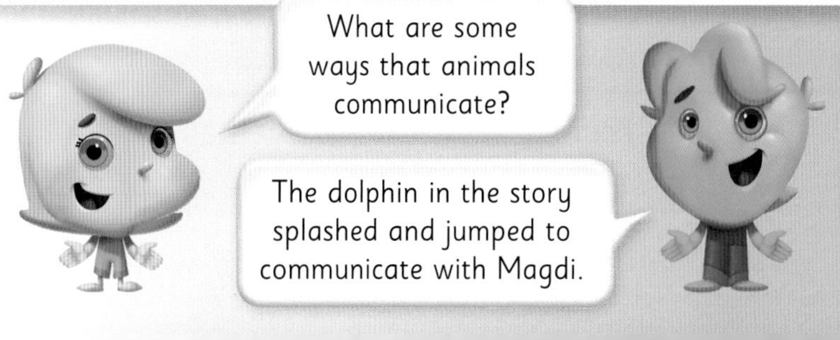

Get Ready

Words

A Listen and say the words. Then read and listen to the sentences. 2•09

communicative | locate | collaborate | imitate | behave | indicate | attract | threaten | defend | approach | express | produce

1 Dolphins are **communicative** animals. They use sounds and movement.
2 Whales **locate** each other by singing songs.
3 I **collaborate** with my classmates on projects.
4 Parrots often **imitate** human words.
5 We **behave** well in class!
6 Can you **indicate** on the map where you live?
7 Some birds **attract** a mate by building colorful nests.
8 The rattlesnake **threatens** its enemies by rattling its tail.
9 Animals have ways of **defending** their territory.
10 The lion **approaches** its prey silently.
11 People **express** themselves with their hands when they talk.
12 The sound a tiger **produces** is a growl.

B Match. What other answers can you think of?

1 What animals are dangerous to approach? • • **a** in a doctor's office
2 How can you locate things you lose? • • **b** lions
3 Who are kids communicative with? • • **c** a kitten
4 What baby animal can a person imitate? • • **d** look very carefully
5 Where do patients behave well? • • **e** a snake
6 What long animal threatens its prey? • • **f** friends

C Choose the best word to complete each sentence.

attracted collaborate defend express indicate produces

1 Do you ______________ with other students on school projects?
2 I can ______________ where I live on a map.
3 Bees are ______________ to flowers.
4 We can ______________ that we are happy with words.
5 A scared animal will ______________ itself.
6 A tiger ______________ a loud growl.

Before You Read

Think Which animals have you learned about so far? How do they communicate?

D **Learn** Asking Questions

When you read, it's good to ask yourself questions. Questions help you understand what you're reading. Here are some examples:

- What is the main idea?
- Why do animals communicate?
- How does an elephant use its trunk?

Read the text and ask questions about it. Use *why*, *what*, and *how*.

People communicate in many different ways. We use words to say how we feel. Sometimes, we use words to say what we know and to give other people information.

We often communicate with our gestures. The next time you're talking to a friend, look at your hands. What are you doing with them?

People also communicate the way they feel through their faces. Look at these pictures. How do these people feel?

E **Words in Context** Scan the article on pages 80–81 and circle these words. As you read, try to guess what the words mean.

underwater **decibels** **territory** **alarm** **signals** **difficulty**

F Look at the pictures on pages 80–81. Make a list of the animals you already know. Say what other animals you think you will learn about.

PREVIEW

Chatterboxes

In this *article*, you will learn that animals communicate to defend territory, find food, and for many other reasons. An article provides interesting facts about a topic. Articles often appear in magazines and newspapers. As you read, ask questions about the text. This will help you to understand what you're reading.

Life Science

Read 2·10

Chatterboxes

Do you think animals can communicate? No? Think again! There are three main types of animal communication, and they all happen for different reasons.

Communication Between Animals of the Same Species

Defending Territory and Attracting a Mate

Hippos communicate underwater and on land, but mostly they communicate underwater by making noises called grunts and bellows. On land, the volume of their bellows can reach 115 decibels. That's as loud as thunder or a jet plane! They communicate with each other to defend their territory, which is their own space. Hippos bellow when they fight other hippos and when they want to attract a mate.

Food

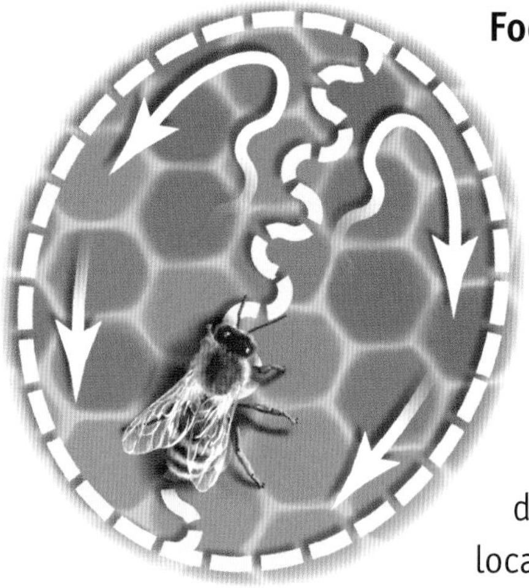

Honeybees dance to communicate.

Honeybees do a special kind of dance called the waggle dance when they find nectar, water, or pollen. The dance is like a map of their journey. The dance helps other bees locate the nectar, water, or pollen.

Think

What are two reasons that animals communicate?

Danger!

Most animals have predators that want to kill and eat them. Lions, cheetahs, and eagles prey on vervet monkeys, so the monkeys have alarm signals for each predator. Rabbits thump their powerful back paws on the ground to warn other rabbits of danger. Beavers slap their tails hard against the water to scare away foxes and alligators.

When vervet monkeys hear the lion or cheetah signal, they climb trees to protect themselves. When they hear the eagle signal, they hide on the forest floor.

Communication Between Animals of Different Species

Warning!

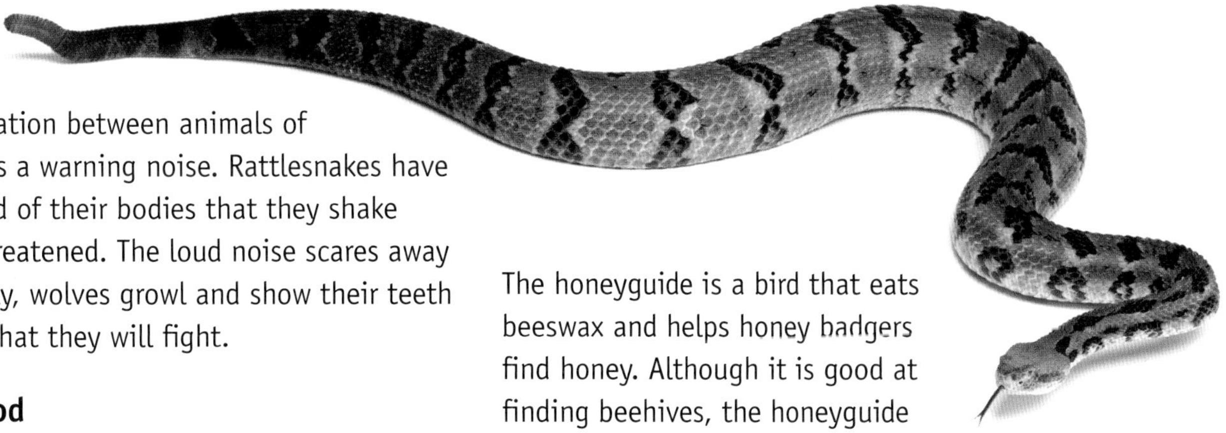

The most common kind of communication between animals of different species is a warning noise. Rattlesnakes have a rattle on the end of their bodies that they shake when they feel threatened. The loud noise scares away predators. Similarly, wolves growl and show their teeth to warn enemies that they will fight.

Food

A type of lizard, called a *gecko*, and an insect, called a *treehopper*, cooperate with each other. They both eat honeydew, a sweet, sticky liquid that comes from trees. The gecko sees the treehopper vibrating its stomach, so it knows that the treehopper is eating honeydew. The gecko shakes its head to indicate to the treehopper that it wants honeydew. The treehopper throws honeydew toward the gecko, which catches it in its mouth. Why does the hopper do this? It's possible that the gecko protects the hopper from predators.

The honeyguide is a bird that eats beeswax and helps honey badgers find honey. Although it is good at finding beehives, the honeyguide has difficulty getting into the hives. The honey badger eats honey, but it has trouble finding hives, and so these two animals collaborate. The honeyguide makes noises and flaps its wings to attract a honey badger. Once the honey badger has climbed a tree and broken open the hive, it eats the honey, and the honeyguide gets to eat, too!

Think

What are different ways animals communicate?

Communication Between Humans and Animals

Dolphins, apes, and parrots are the animals that have communicated the most with humans. A famous bonobo ape, Kanzi, was the first non-human to learn language the way a child does, by listening and observing. A scientist said that Kanzi had learned 450 words using a keyboard. He also told us that Kanzi was learning new things every day.

Alex was a grey parrot who, like most parrots, could imitate words, but he could also identify objects, colors, and shapes. He died when he was 31. His last words to his trainer, Dr. Pepperberg, were: "You be good. I love you." Dr. Pepperberg said Alex had started to learn the alphabet. Every time Alex got a letter right, he told Dr. Pepperberg that he wanted a nut!

Understand

Comprehension

Think Were you surprised by any of the information in "Chatterboxes"? Tell your partner two surprising facts you learned.

A Choose an animal from the article. Use the chart to answer questions about it.

Asking Questions About Animal Communication

Animal	
Where?	
When?	
Why?	
How?	

B Circle the correct answer.

1 Hippos communicate ____

- **a** underwater and on land.
- **b** only underwater.
- **c** only on land.
- **d** only with people.

2 Honeybees communicate with ____

- **a** grunts and bellows.
- **b** growls and roars.
- **c** a dance.
- **d** a song.

3 Vervet monkeys have alarm signals to ____

- **a** tell each other about the weather.
- **b** tell each other about food.
- **c** tell each other about their territory.
- **d** tell each other about danger.

4 Kanzi the ape and Alex the parrot worked with ____

- **a** honey badgers.
- **b** scientists.
- **c** snakes.
- **d** rabbits.

C **Words in Context** Look again at the words you circled in the article. Then match the words to the definitions.

1 territory
2 decibel
3 signal
4 alarm
5 difficulty
6 underwater

- **a** an area that an animal has as its own
- **b** a situation that is hard to deal with
- **c** something used to share information
- **d** below the surface of water
- **e** to make something feel afraid or worried
- **f** a measurement of how loud sound is

Workbook Grammar pages 74–75

Grammar in Use

D **Listen and read along. Then write the letter of the correct answer.** 2•11

1 Which sentence is in direct speech? ______

2 Which sentence is in reported speech? ______

a I asked how many words Kanzi was learning.

b How many words is Kanzi learning?

E **Learn Grammar** Reported Speech with *Told* or *Asked*

Remember: Use **said that** to report what someone said. You can also use **told** or **asked**. After *told* or *asked*, you need to add an object pronoun or someone's name.

Don't forget, if the direct speech is in the present tense, the reported speech changes to past tense.

Reported Speech

He told us that Kanzi was learning new things every day.
A classmate asked the scientist what Kanzi was learning.

Rewrite the sentences in your notebook. Change direct speech to reported speech. Change reported speech to direct speech.

1. She said that she was learning about animal communication.
2. "I'm going to the park," she said.
3. "I'm studying about crocodiles in school," he told me.
4. I asked my father what time it was.

F **Follow the instructions and write each person's name.**

Walk around the classroom and find someone who ...
1 is interested in wild animals.
2 wants to know more about snakes.

G **Use reported speech to share what you learned with your partner.**

Communicate

Listening

Think What are the biggest mammals you can name? Can you guess what animal weighs between 4 and 7 tons?

A Listen. What animal do you think makes this sound? 2•12

B Listen again and circle the correct answers. There is more than one correct answer for each question. 2•13

1 Elephants use their trunks to ____

- **a** listen and clap.
- **b** hide from other elephants.
- **c** know where other elephants are.
- **d** touch and smell.

2 Elephants use their ears to ____

- **a** show excitement or happiness.
- **b** touch and smell.
- **c** cool down.
- **d** make sounds.

3 Elephants use their voices to ____

- **a** make sounds that humans can't hear.
- **b** communicate over several kilometers.
- **c** communicate over 1,000 kilometers.
- **d** make sounds that humans can hear.

Speaking 2•14

C Summarize what you've learned.

Write down five or six facts you learned about animals in this unit. Talk about what you've learned.

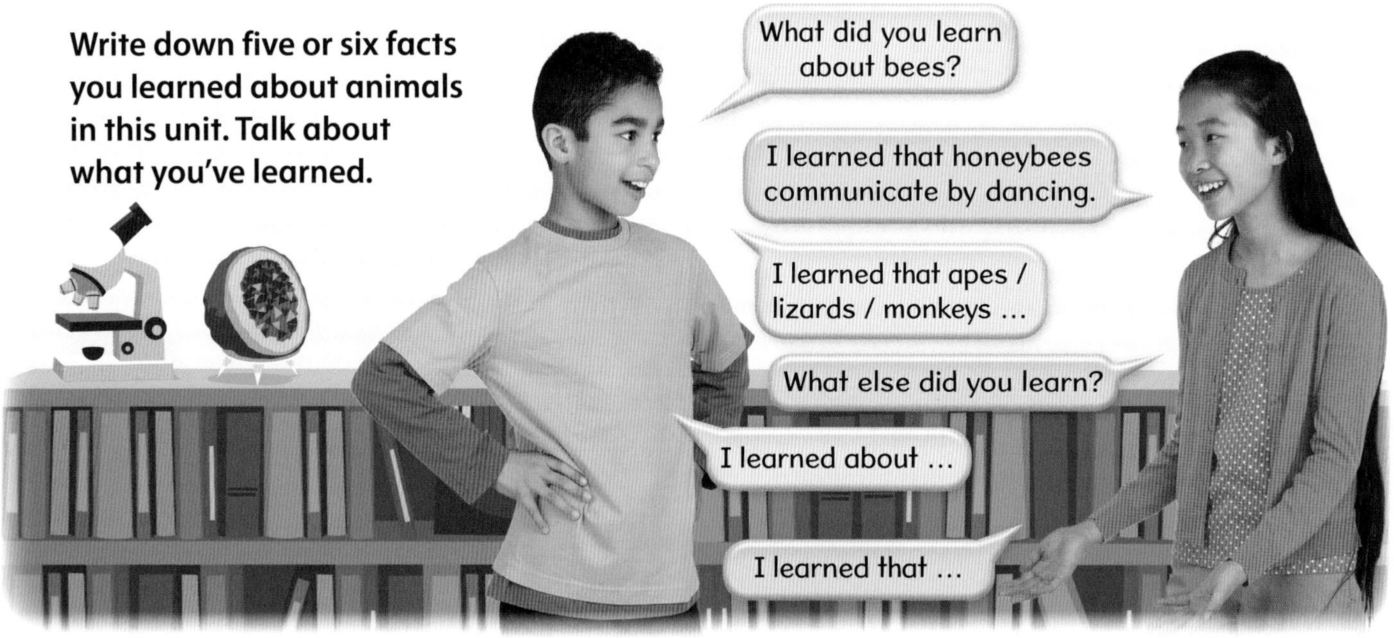

Word Study

D **Learn** Suffix *-ion*

Remember: A suffix is added to the end of a word. It can change the part of speech from a verb to a noun.

Elephants communicate in many different ways. (verb)
Animal communication is fascinating. (noun)

Listen and say the words. Write the words by adding *-ion*. If a verb ends in an *e* cross out the last letter. 2•15 A-Z

1 connect ______________________ 5 decorate ______________________

2 locate ______________________ 6 collaborate ______________________

3 prevent ______________________ 7 migrate ______________________

4 educate ______________________ 8 protect ______________________

E **Work with your partner. Write a sentence using each verb above. Then write a sentence with each noun you made by adding the suffix *-ion*.**

Writing Study

F **Learn** Pronoun Agreement

Remember: A pronoun matches its noun. If the noun is singular, the pronoun and the verb are singular. If the noun is plural, the pronoun and the verb are plural.

The girl is watching a movie. She likes it.
The boys are playing music. They are making a lot of noise!

The words **everybody**, **anybody**, **nobody**, and **somebody** are singular.

Everybody likes chocolate. (Not: Everybody like chocolate.)

Complete these sentences. Use the correct form of the verb in parentheses.

1 ______________ (do) anybody want to go to the movies with me?

2 Everybody ______________ (like) the new teacher.

3 Nobody ______________ (want) to go out in the rain.

Write Now practice writing in the **Workbook**. page 77

Wrap Up

Writing

A Read this descriptive essay.

Interesting starting sentence

Introduction with descriptive adjectives

Last year, I saw a huge octopus in a tank at the zoo. It had a large head and eight long arms with round suckers on them. While I was watching, the octopus changed its skin color. At first, it was brown with white spots. Then it moved near some pink coral, and it changed its color to pink. It almost disappeared into the coral. A scientist at the zoo said that the octopus is a very intelligent animal.

Body

When I got home, I read more about octopuses. Most octopuses live on the bottom of the ocean or in coral reefs. They eat crabs, shrimps, and lobsters. An octopus uses its suckers to hold its prey and pull it into its mouth. If an octopus loses an arm, it can grow a new one. When it wants to move fast, it propels itself by making jets of water with its body. An octopus has good eyesight and can see colors.

An octopus changes its skin color to communicate with other octopuses. Its skin color can attract a mate or warn other octopuses to stay away. Some octopuses use colors to show their moods. When they're white, they're afraid. When they're red, they're angry. When they're brown, they're relaxed.

Conclusion

I think octopuses are very smart and can do many interesting things! I want to go back to the zoo to see the octopus again. I hope that one day I can see an octopus in the ocean.

B Answer the questions.

1 How does the writer start the essay?
2 How does the writer finish the essay?
3 What words does the writer use to describe the octopus?

C **Learn** Writing a Descriptive Essay

- Choose a topic that interests you for your essay.
- Write a sentence in your first paragraph to clearly state your topic.
- Use adjectives to describe people, animals, or things.
- Draw and label some pictures to share with the class. It will help make your descriptions more interesting.
- Finish your essay with something that reminds the reader of how you started it.

Write Now go to the **Workbook** to plan and write your own descriptive essay. page 79

D Present your descriptive essay to the class.

1 Tell the class what topic you wrote about.
2 Tell why you chose that topic.
3 Allow the class to look at your pictures while you read your essay.
4 Read your essay with energy. Try to make your descriptions come to life.

BIG QUESTION 4

How do animals communicate?

A Watch the video. How do you see animals communicating?

B What are some answers to the Big Question? Talk about them with your partner.

C Complete the **Big Question Chart**. Then discuss it with the class.

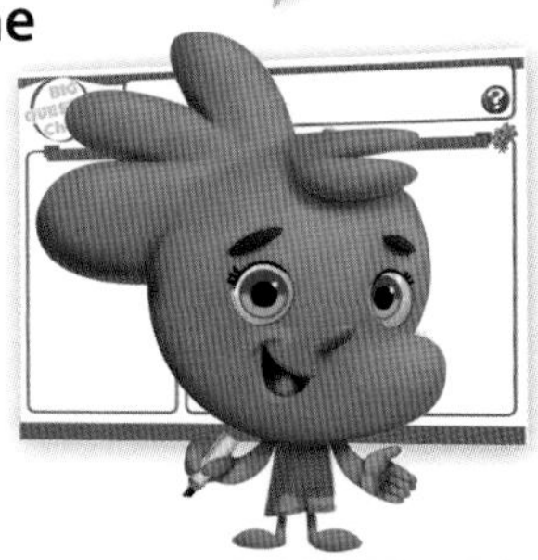

In units
9 and 10
you will:

WATCH
a video about different countries.

LEARN
what different cultures give us.

READ
about cultures and a girl in a new country.

WRITE a travel brochure.

PRESENT your brochure to the class.

BIG QUESTION 5

What do different cultures give to the world?

A **Watch the video. Then talk about it with your partner.**

B **Look at the picture and discuss it with your class.**

1. What was this place used for long ago?
2. How old do you think the building is?

C **Think and answer the questions.**

1. Where do you live?
2. Have you ever been to another country? Where?
3. What is your country famous for?
4. What things do you use that come from other countries?

D **Discuss this topic with your class. Fill out the Big Question Chart.**

UNIT 9 Get Ready

Words

A Listen and say the words. Then read and listen to the sentences. 2•16

culture | civilization | contribution | development | achievement | device | process | tradition | custom | benefit | ceremony | product

1 Art and music are important parts of a country's **culture**.
2 Cairo was at the center of one of the world's oldest **civilizations**.
3 One of China's **contributions** to the world was the compass.
4 The use of papyrus led to the **development** of paper.
5 Good job! Passing the exam is a great **achievement**.
6 My grandfather has a **device** that monitors his heart rate.
7 Growing trees is a slow **process**.
8 A yearly New Year celebration is a **tradition**.
9 Taking your shoes off before entering a house is a Japanese **custom**.
10 We **benefit** from inventions because they make our lives easier.
11 The couple said vows during their wedding **ceremony**.
12 A **product** is anything that you can sell.

B Choose the best word to complete each sentence.

achievement product device traditions process benefit ceremony

1 Winning a race is an ________________.
2 What holiday ________________ do you have in your country?
3 I went to my brother's high school graduation ________________.
4 Our class decided that cookies would be a good ________________ to sell.
5 A pencil sharpener is a ________________ that most students use.
6 Students ________________ from studying hard.
7 A recipe tells you the ________________ for making a cake.

C Circle the one that doesn't belong.

1 civilization people ocean
2 culture arts device
3 process gift contribution
4 decrease development creation
5 custom product tradition
6 benefit help custom
7 Earth device tool
8 product source object

Before You Read

Think Why do people invent things?

D **Learn** Main Idea and Details

When you read a text, think about the **main idea**. The main idea is the most important point of the text. Then think about the **details**. Ask yourself these questions:

- What is the main idea in the text?
- What details support the main idea?

Read the paragraph. Then fill in the organizer.

Whiteboards

Do you ever wonder where the things you use every day come from? For example, think about the dry erase whiteboard. This simple device is a very important invention. The whiteboard has been used since the 1960s. It became more popular in the 1990s, and today whiteboards are in thousands of offices, meeting rooms, and classrooms around the world. What would we do without whiteboards?

Main Idea

____

Detail	Detail	Detail
______________	______________	______________
______________	______________	______________

E **Words in Context** Scan the narrative on pages 92–93 and circle these words. As you read, try to guess what the words mean.

trade tablets voyage ancient advanced tools

F **Answer these questions before you read.**

1 Do you know where chocolate came from?
2 How do people get from one place to another?

PREVIEW

Journey Back in Time

In this *historical narrative*, you'll learn about things that came from different countries. A historical narrative tells the true story of things that happened. It always has facts and sometimes has pictures and maps. As you read, think about the main idea and details.

Social Studies: History

Read 2-17

Journey Back in Time

Imagine traveling back in time! Who do you see? Who sees you? Where would you go? What amazing things might you discover there? Many countries have made contributions to our modern life. Some have invented things; others have given us art, music, and stories.

Mesopotamia

You start your journey in ancient Mesopotamia. That's a place we now call Iraq. Mesopotamia was between two huge rivers: the Euphrates and the Tigris. The people there needed good boats to travel on these rivers so they could explore and trade. So, five thousand years ago, the Mesopotamians invented a new type of sailboat. Their design is still being used today! One of these sailboats can take you to many different places along the route of your journey.

Think
What's the main idea?

Before you leave Mesopotamia, be sure to visit a city called Sumer. Many things were invented there. What Sumerian invention can you take on your journey? Their most important invention was something you can take with you anywhere: writing! The Mesopotamians in Sumer found a way to make pictures on clay tablets (flat pieces of clay) to tell a story.

Writing isn't the only contribution the Mesopotamians made to the world. People also believe the wheel was invented there. The Mesopotamians put wooden rollers under carts so that they could transport goods and people more easily. Today we benefit from the invention of wheels in everything from watches to airplanes.

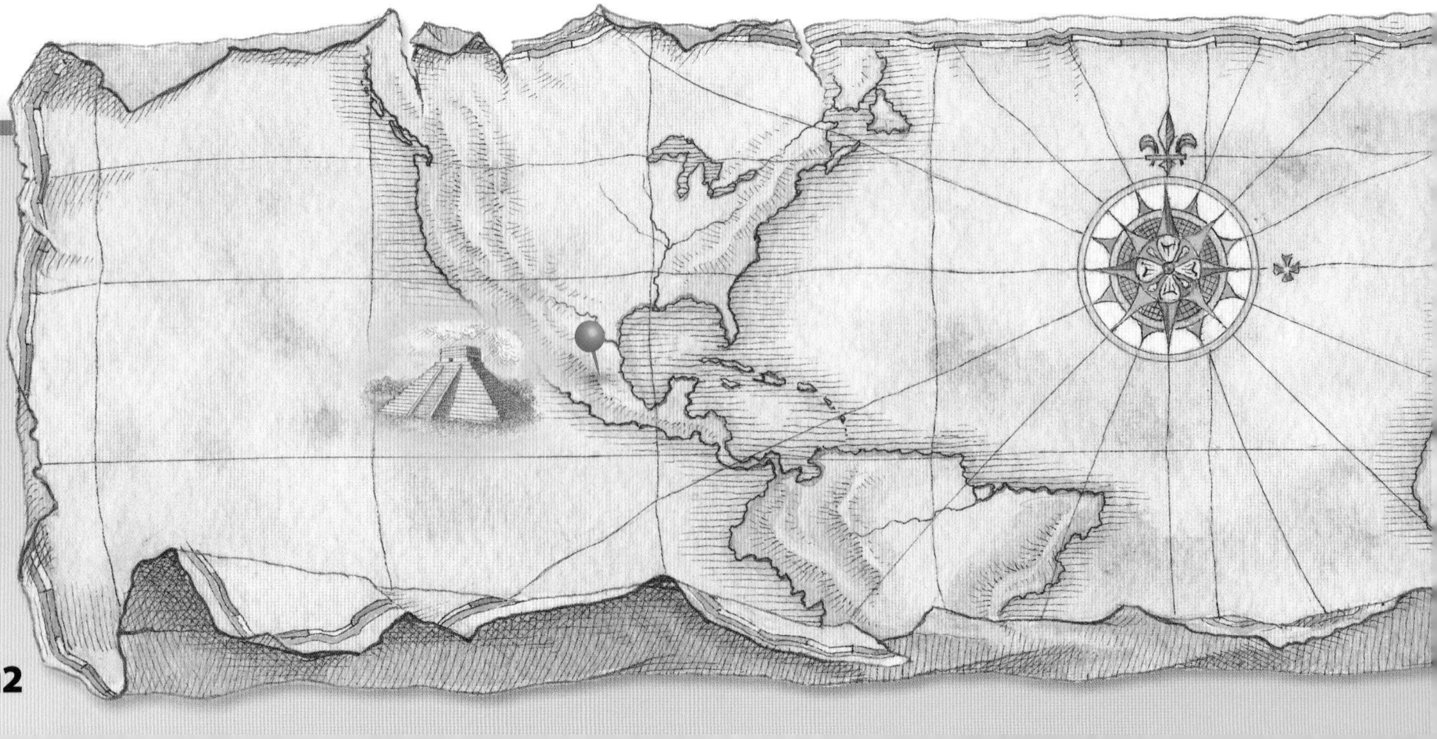

Egypt

From the Tigris River, you sail all the way to the Mediterranean Sea. Now you can see the coast of Egypt. The Egyptians were very good at math, medicine, architecture, and sculpture. They had a rich culture of art, music, and a form of writing called hieroglyphics. They learned to make paper from a plant called papyrus. Because we use paper instead of Sumerian clay tablets, today we have books, magazines, and newspapers.

China

The next country you visit cannot be reached by sailboat. China is over 5,000 miles away from Egypt. You will be tired when you reach China, but your trip is not finished. You have one more long voyage to make across the Pacific Ocean. Luckily, the Chinese have invented a device called a compass. This is a very important invention. It helps you find your way on land or sea by always pointing to the north. It was originally invented to help Chinese sailors navigate. Now we have compasses on our cell phones and in our cars, so no one needs to get lost.

Mexico

Using your compass, you can sail all the way across the Pacific Ocean to Mexico. There, you will explore another ancient civilization: the Maya. This was a very advanced civilization with many interesting customs and traditions. The Maya created and discovered many important things using only very simple tools. They were excellent astronomers and mathematicians. They developed a written language using hieroglyphs, and they built huge pyramids and sculptures. The Maya produced many different goods, including tools, jewelry, and cloth. They also made a new kind of drink by mixing cocoa beans with spices, water, and chilies. They used the drink in special ceremonies and to make people healthy. Though the special Mayan drink tasted bitter, what they made was actually a kind of chocolate. Until the Maya invented it, no one had ever tasted chocolate before.

You have sailed on a Sumerian boat, found your way with a Chinese compass, and you can write all about your journey on some Egyptian papyrus!

Think
What details support the main idea?

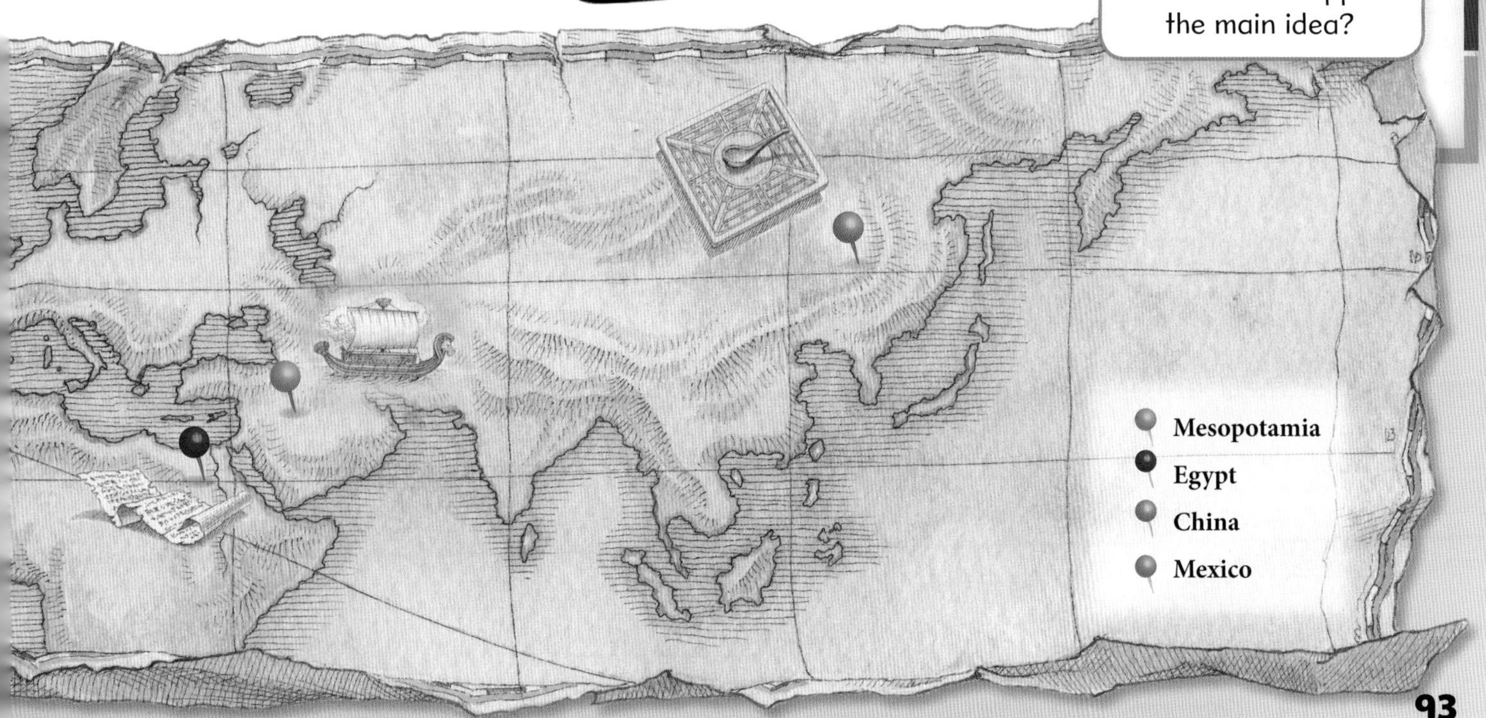

Comprehension

Think Talk with your partner about three things you learned from "Journey Back in Time." Which countries did you already know about?

A Fill in the organizer with information from the historical narrative. Then discuss what you wrote with your partner.

Main Idea

____

Detail	Detail	Detail	Detail
____________	____________	____________	____________
____________	____________	____________	____________
____________	____________	____________	____________

B Answer the questions.

1 What three things did the ancient Mesopotamians invent?
2 Where was paper invented?
3 Why is a compass important?
4 What ingredients do you need to make Mayan hot chocolate?
5 What do you think is the most important invention in the narrative? Why?

C **Words in Context** Look again at the words you circled in the narrative. Then write them in the correct sentences.

1 Telescopes and microscopes are good ______________ for studying things.
2 Archeologists found an ______________ statue in the desert.
3 A ______________ usually takes a long time, especially on the sea.
4 Before there was paper, people carved letters on wooden or clay ______________.
5 Countries all around the world ______________ with each other.
6 Modern compass systems are much more ______________ than the early compass.

Workbook Grammar
pages 86–87

Grammar in Use

D **Listen and read along. Then circle the correct answer.** 2•18

1 Who did Finn see? **a** nobody **b** many people

2 Who saw Finn? **a** nobody **b** Finn's mom

E **Learn Grammar** Asking Questions

Remember: Ask questions with **who**, **where**, **when**, **why**, **what**, **which**, and **how**.

Be careful! There's a difference between these two questions:

Question	Answer
Who saw Finn? (*Who* is the subject.)	**Finn's mom saw Finn.**
Who did Finn see? (*Who* is the object.)	**Finn didn't see anybody.**

Read the situations. Check (✓) the best question to ask the person.

1 Your brother or sister wrote an e-mail.
☐ Who did you write to? ☐ Who wrote to you?

2 You go to a friend's house, and your friend is watching TV.
☐ Who's watching you? ☐ What are you watching?

3 Your classmate got help with a difficult math problem.
☐ Who did you help? ☐ Who helped you?

4 Your friend tells you he's going to travel with his family.
☐ Who are you traveling with? ☐ Where are you going?

F **Work with your partner. Take turns asking and answering questions about what you did yesterday. Use all of the question words.**

Communicate

Listening

Think Where did the Olympic Games first start? What do you know about the Olympics?

A **Learn** Listening for Facts

Listen for facts. Facts are things that are true.
Greece is a country in Europe.

An opinion is how you feel or think about someone or something.
I think running is fun.

Listen. What country does the girl come from? 2•19

B **Listen again. Circle Yes or No.** 2•20

1	The Olympic Games started in Athens.	Yes	No
2	The Olympic Games are named after the city of Olympia.	Yes	No
3	The Olympic Games started 1,000 years ago.	Yes	No
4	The race in the Olympic Games was 170 meters.	Yes	No
5	The runners wore sneakers for the race.	Yes	No
6	The Greeks invented the Olympic Games.	Yes	No

Speaking 2•21

C **Take turns asking and telling about an invention you think is important. Remember to ask using all of the question words.**

- who
- what
- when
- where
- why
- which
- how

Word Study

D **Learn** Word Roots

Some words in English have roots from Latin or Greek.

Root	Meaning	Example
cent (Latin)	one hundred	centimeter
circum (Latin)	around	circumstance
bio (Greek)	life	biology
tele (Greek)	far away	telephone

Listen and say the words. Circle the word roots. Then work with a partner to use each word in a sentence. 2•22 A-Z

1 centipede	**2** centigrade	**3** antibiotic	**4** telecommunication
5 centimeter	**6** biologist	**7** circumstance	**8** telephone

Writing Study

E **Learn** Using Parentheses

You can use parentheses to give extra information in a sentence. The information in parentheses isn't necessary to understand the sentence.

Jorge (Luke's friend) is coming over to our house tonight.

Put parentheses in the correct places in the sentences.

1. Beethoven 1770–1827 was a famous German composer.
2. We saw the black vehicle a truck leaving at high speed.
3. Mr. Sonn my math teacher lives near my house.
4. Madrid the capital of Spain is a beautiful city.

Write Now practice writing in the **Workbook**. page 89

BIG QUESTION 5

What do different cultures give to the world?

UNIT 10 Get Ready

Words

A **Listen and say the words. Then read and listen to the sentences.** 2•23

delicious	creamy	spicy	nutty	ladle	sticky
crunchy	runny	smooth	whirring	booming	spot

1 Bananas are **delicious**. I could eat them every day.
2 This ice cream is very **creamy**.
3 Chilies and peppers are **spicy**. They make food taste hot.
4 Mom made some **nutty** cookies. They had walnuts in them.
5 The baker **ladled** milk into the flour and butter mixture.
6 My hands are **sticky** from eating candy.
7 When someone bites a **crunchy** apple, you can hear the noise.
8 The butter is **runny** because it's been in the sun.
9 Mix the ingredients until they're **smooth**.
10 What's that **whirring** noise? It sounds like a washing machine.
11 The captain's **booming** voice can be heard all over the ship.
12 Did you **spot** any mistakes in my homework?

B **Write the words in the correct sentences.**

spicy smooth booming whirring nutty ladle spot

1 My father has a ______________ voice. You can hear him from far away!

2 Mix the chocolate until it's ______________ and then add some almonds to make it ______________. ______________ the mixture into a bowl.

3 The car is making a strange ______________ noise. Help me ______________ a gas station.

4 The food was so hot and ______________ that I burned my tongue!

C **What answers can you think of?**

1 What foods are crunchy?	
2 What foods are runny?	
3 What foods are creamy?	
4 What foods are delicious?	
5 What foods are sticky?	

Before You Read

Think **What countries have you learned about so far? What did they contribute to the world?**

D **Learn** Visualizing

When you read, make pictures in your mind. This helps you understand what you're reading. It also helps you remember stories more easily. Ask these questions:

- What do the characters look like?
- Do any characters remind you of someone you know?
- Where is the story set? What does it look like there?
- Have you ever been to a place like this?

Read the short story. Tell your partner what you see in your mind. Then answer the questions.

Ricky was small and thin. He didn't like being in the strange house all alone. He decided to leave. He tiptoed slowly down the dark corridor. He was breathing hard and felt very anxious. Suddenly, there was a small scratching noise. Ricky's heart began to beat loudly. Then he saw a huge insect. It had enormous eyes, long hairy legs, and a pink tongue as long as Ricky's arm.

1 What does Ricky look like?
2 Where is he?
3 What does the insect look like?
4 Is the insect scary or funny?

E **Words in Context** **Scan the story on pages 100–101 and circle these words. As you read, try to guess what the words mean.**

square **skidded** **dizzy** **sniffing** **molds** **winked**

F **Answer the questions before you read.**

1 What is your favorite sweet?
2 What do you know about chocolate?
3 Look at the pictures on pages 100–101. Where do you think this story takes place?

PREVIEW

Choco Choco Boom Boom!

In this *fantasy* story, you'll read about a girl who goes back in time. A fantasy is a story that couldn't happen in real life. Like other stories, it has a plot, characters, and a setting. As you read, make pictures in your mind to help you understand and remember the story.

Read 2•24

Choco Choco Boom Boom!

The wheels on the train seemed to be talking to Akiko. They made a rhythmic, whirring noise: Choco boom boom, choco choco boom boom, choco boom boom.

"Brussels. Capital of Belgium. Next stop!" said the guard in a booming voice. "Is this your stop?" he asked.

"Yes, it is," replied Akiko excitedly. "Chocolate City!"

Akiko loved chocolate, but what she wanted to taste most of all was Belgian chocolate. Everyone said that it was the best chocolate in the world.

Akiko glanced quickly at her map and ran down a long street. The air was full of delicious smells, creamy, nutty smells. Akiko breathed deeply. Soon, she thought, she would find a store and she would buy a selection of Belgian chocolates.

Akiko turned a corner. In front of her, there was a palace belonging to the King and Queen of Belgium. Looking up at the roof, Akiko spotted a black, yellow, and red flag, and beyond the palace, a big town square. *Maybe I'll find my chocolate there*, she thought.

As Akiko skidded into the square, she couldn't believe her eyes. All around her, there were massive buildings decorated with statues and flower sellers were selling red, yellow, and white flowers.

"Excuse me," Akiko said to a man selling French fries. "Is there a chocolate store near here?"

"Yes, there is," laughed the man. "There's one right down that street. It makes the crunchiest chocolate in town."

Akiko zoomed straight into the store. Her heart was pounding: Choco boom boom, choco choco boom boom.

Think
Visualize what the city square looks like.

“May I please have five of your best chocolates?” Akiko asked the man behind the counter.

“Of course,” he replied, selecting the chocolates. “And this extra one,” he said, handing her a perfectly round chocolate, “is extremely special. It’s called a praline.”

Akiko closed her eyes and bit the chocolate exactly in half. Everything went dark and she felt slightly dizzy. Her heart was racing again: Choco boom boom, choco choco boom boom. She opened her eyes, and to her astonishment she saw a strange kitchen with a large stove, a wooden table, and shiny pots and pans everywhere. Stirring chocolate in one of the pots was a man who looked just like the man in the store, but he was wearing strange, old-fashioned clothes. “Welcome,” he said softly. “I’ve been expecting you.”

Akiko approached the man, sniffing the delicious smells around her.

“Do you smell that?” he whispered. “It’s a praline, my latest invention. People will love it!”

Akiko was confused. Pralines had been invented in 1912 by someone called Jean Neuhaus. Unless … that was it! The special praline she’d bitten in half had taken her back in time! And the man standing before her was the famous Jean Neuhaus.

“Let’s make some,” said Jean. Together, Jean and Akiko mixed butter, sugar, chocolate, and almonds and ladled it into small molds to set. Akiko was the happiest she’d been in her life. Not only had she tasted Belgian chocolates, but now she knew the recipe for pralines.

“Time to go now,” said Jean as he poured out the last drop of chocolate. “You know what to do, don’t you?”

“Yes, I do,” said Akiko. And she swallowed the other half of the praline she’d been given.

Everything went dark again, and the dizziness Akiko had felt earlier returned. Choco boom boom, choco choco boom boom went her heart, and suddenly there she was, back in the store. The man behind the counter winked at her, and with a big smile he said, “Never forget. Belgian chocolate is the very best in the world.”

Understand

Comprehension

Think Choose two things you liked about "Choco Choco Boom Boom!" and discuss them with your partner.

A Talk with your partner about the pictures in the story. Were the pictures the same or different from what you visualized? What else can you visualize that is not in the pictures?

B Circle the correct answer.

1 Akiko travels to Belgium by ____
- **a** car.
- **b** bus.
- **c** train.
- **d** plane.

2 Akiko finds chocolate ____
- **a** in a store.
- **b** in a square.
- **c** in a palace.
- **d** on a statue.

3 When Akiko bit the praline in half she felt ____
- **a** sick.
- **b** dizzy.
- **c** hungry.
- **d** tired.

4 Jean Neuhaus invented ____
- **a** Belgian pralines.
- **b** Almonds.
- **c** French fries.
- **d** molds.

C **Words in Context** Look again at the words you circled in the story. Then match each word to its definition.

1 square	a moved or slid sideways
2 skidded	b feeling as if everything is spinning
3 sniffing	c containers that you pour a liquid in to set
4 dizzy	d making a sound by breathing through your nose
5 molds	e closed and opened one eye quickly
6 winked	f an open space in a city that has buildings all around it

Workbook Grammar pages 94–95

Grammar in Use

D **Listen and read along. Then circle the correct answer.** 2•25

Which answer is more polite? **a** Yes. **b** Yes, I do!

E **Learn Grammar** Short Answers

Remember: Short answers include **Yes, I am**; **No, he didn't**; **Yes, they can**; **No, we won't**; and **Yes, there is**. Using a short answer is more polite than answering only **Yes** or **No**. Some examples of short answers are:

Question	Short Answer
Is there a chocolate shop near here?	**Yes, there is.**
Do you like my new sneakers?	**Yes, I do!**
Has it stopped raining?	**No, it hasn't.**

Work with your partner. Take turns asking and answering with short answers.

1 Do you like sports?
2 Did you have pizza for dinner last night?
3 Can you snowboard?
4 Are you 15 years old?
5 Did your family ever go to Belgium?
6 Did you ever act in a play?
7 Is your favorite color blue?
8 Have you ever made chocolate?

F **Work with your partner. Ask questions about your daily lives. Use short answers.**

Communicate

Listening

Think **Why do we have umbrellas? Which country do you think invented the umbrella?**

A Listen to the conversation. Circle the correct answers. 2•26

1 Umbrellas first came from ____

a Japan. **b** Korea. **c** China.

2 They were invented ____

a 1,700 years ago. **b** 700 years ago. **c** 17 years ago.

3 A ____ can make its own umbrella.

a donkey **b** monkey **c** elephant

4 The Chinese made umbrellas out of ____

a wood and metal. **b** plastic and rubber. **c** paper and bamboo.

B Listen again. What do monkeys use to make umbrellas? 2•27

Speaking 2•28

C Learn Making Suggestions

When you make suggestions, use **Why don't we … ?**; **Should we … ?**; **Let's …** ; **How about… ?**

To respond, say **That's a great idea**; **OK, let's do that**; or **Yes, I'd love to.** Or **No, that's OK**; **No, thanks**; **Not this time**; **maybe another time.**

Talk with your partner. Take turns suggesting these activities.

- **go to a movie**
- **have a snack**
- **watch a TV show**
- **go to the mall**

Word Study

D **Learn** Suffix *-ous*

Remember: A suffix is added to the end of a word. The suffix -ous can change a word from a noun to an adjective. This changes the meaning of the word.

fame + ous = famous

The man standing before her was the famous Jean Neuhaus.

Listen, say, and number the words. 2•29 A-Z

____adventurous ____envious

____carnivorous ____venomous

____spacious ____mountainous

____humorous ____marvelous

E **Work with your partner. Write a noun for each adjective in D. Write sentences with the nouns and adjectives.**

Writing Study

F **Learn** Giving Examples

Use for example, for instance, and such as to explain your ideas. Notice where the commas are placed.

There are many ways to keep fit, for example, swimming, jogging, or playing a sport.

I can play several instruments, for instance, the guitar, the piano, and the recorder.

We learn many things at school, such as music, art, and history.

Correct the punctuation in the sentences.

1 Maria can play many team sports such as basketball, baseball, and soccer.
2 I like many different vegetables for example peas, cabbage, and carrots.
3 My aunt has a lot of interests such as reading, singing, and traveling.
4 They visited several places for instance Korea, Turkey, Jordan, and Mexico.

Write Now practice writing in the **Workbook.** page 97

Wrap Up

Writing

A Read this travel brochure.

Welcoming message

Visit Brazil! It's a fantastic country full of sights, culture, and great food.

Things to See and Do

First point

First, you can visit the Amazon forest, in the north of Brazil. It's the biggest tropical forest in the world. It's nine times bigger than Italy! In the Amazon, there are snakes, jaguars, crocodiles, and sloths. There are many species of birds, too, including the toucan.

Second point

Next, you can visit some of our famous cities, like Rio de Janeiro or São Paolo. Many people think Rio is the most beautiful city in Brazil. It's mountainous, but it also has beaches. The people are very friendly. You'll love it!

Third point

Then, why don't you explore some Brazilian culture? We have beautiful buildings. Portuguese people built many of these buildings 300 years ago. You can also see Brazilian art and listen to Brazilian music.

Conclusion

Finally, you can discover some Brazilian traditions and customs. The most famous tradition is the carnival in Rio. People dress in amazing costumes and dance in the street. Or you can go to Boi-Bumbá in Parintins. It's a festival with parades, shows, and Brazilian food. Don't forget to taste the coconut milk. It's delicious!

See you soon in Brazil!

B Answer the questions.

1 How does the writer start the travel brochure?
2 How does the writer organize the information about Brazil?
3 What different things does the writer describe?

C Learn Writing a Travel Brochure

- Start your travel brochure with a welcoming message that makes people want to visit.
- Use transition words (*first*, *next*, *then*, *finally*) to organize what you want to say.
- Describe as many things about the country you've chosen as you can. Talk about the wildlife, cities, customs, traditions, and food.

Write Now go to the **Workbook** to plan and write your own travel brochure. page 99

D Make and present your travel brochure.

1 Choose a location you'd like to visit. Then write your brochure.
2 Draw some pictures to illustrate your travel brochure.
3 Glue your brochure to a large piece of paper.
4 Display the large piece of paper on your classroom wall.
5 Present your travel brochure to a small group.
6 Remember: You want your classmates to visit your country, so make it sound exciting and fun!

BIG QUESTION 5

What do different cultures give to the world?

A **Watch the video. What things do you see from different countries?**

B **What are some answers to the Big Question? Talk about them with your partner.**

C Complete the **Big Question Chart**. Then discuss it with the class.

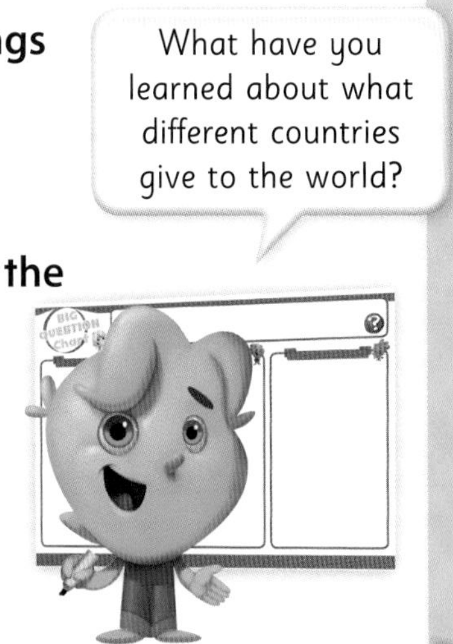

In units **11** and **12** you will:

WATCH
a video about mountains.

LEARN
how mountains give us many things.

READ
a story and an article about mountains.

WRITE a story of your own.

PRESENT your story to the class.

BIG QUESTION 6

Why are mountains important?

A Watch the video. Then talk about it with your partner.

B Look at the picture and discuss it with your class.

1 What lives in the mountains?
2 What is it like at the top or at the bottom of a mountain?

C Think and answer the questions.

1 Where are the world's biggest mountains?
2 Which mountains are nearest to where you live?
3 What can you do in the mountains?
4 Why do you think people climb mountains?

D Discuss this topic with your class. Fill out the **Big Question Chart**.

UNIT 11 Get Ready

Words

A Listen and say the words. Then read and listen to the sentences. 3•02

glacier | mountain range | peak | altitude | valley | steep

slope | hill | terrace | effective | water cycle | vapor

1 When **glaciers** melt, they produce water.
2 The Himalayas are an example of a **mountain range**.
3 The **peak** of Mount Everest is 8,848 meters above sea level.
4 Sometimes it's hard to breathe at high **altitudes**.
5 We hiked from the **valley** to the top of the mountain.
6 The mountain was **steep** and difficult to climb.
7 The girl skied quickly down the **slope**.
8 From the top of the **hill**, we could see our house.
9 To plant rice, farmers carved **terraces** into the mountains.
10 To be **effective**, mountain-climbing ropes must be strong.
11 In the **water cycle**, water evaporates and clouds produce rain.
12 When water boils, we see **vapor**.

B Look at the picture and number the words.

____ mountain range
____ peak
____ slope
____ valley
____ glacier
____ terrace
____ hills

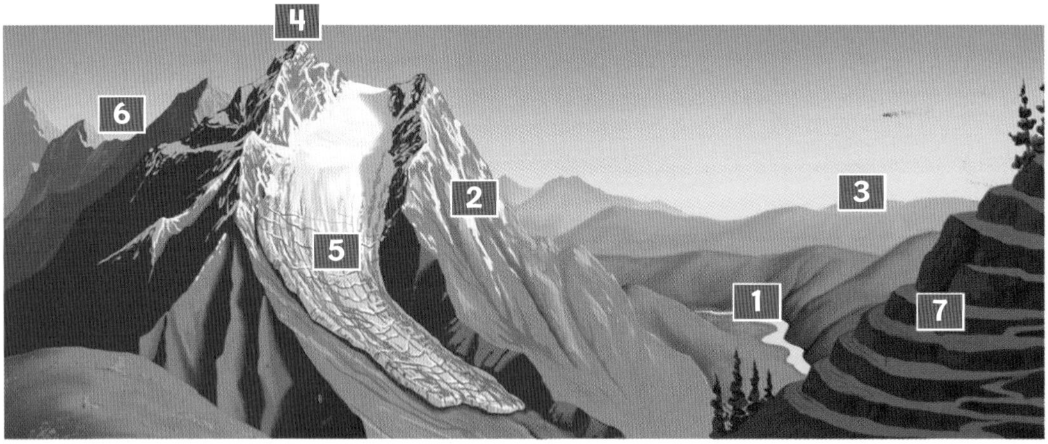

C Circle True (T) or False (F).

1 Stairs can be steep. T F
2 Clouds are in the water cycle. T F
3 A cold soda makes vapor. T F
4 Altitude equals height. T F
5 Some medicines are effective. T F
6 Valleys are higher than peaks. T F

Before You Read

Think Do you eat rice or potatoes? Do you know where they grow?

D **Learn** Cause and Effect

When you read, think about cause and effect. The reason why something happens is the **cause**. What happens as the result of the cause is the **effect**. You can use a cause and effect organizer like the one below to help you.

It was raining. (cause) **I got wet.** (effect)

Read the article. Then fill in the organizer.

Cause and Effect Times

Farmers were very pleased in Australia today. Just the right amounts of rain and sun resulted in an enormous harvest of grain and vegetables. It was the biggest harvest on record.

Meanwhile, in sports, soccer fans were sad to hear that Bucky Goals retired today. Sports experts blamed his injuries from last season for his decision to stop playing.

In the weather, Norwegian teachers closed schools today because 3 meters of snow have fallen there in the past week. Shall we go sledding?

Cause (why something happens)		Effect (what happens)
Three meters of snow fell.	→	Teachers closed schools.
______		______
______		______

E **Words in Context** Scan the text on pages 112–113 and circle these words. As you read, try to guess what the words mean.

transformed **condenses** **released** **flows** **storing** **resources**

F Turn to pages 112–113, and read the headings. What do you think you'll learn about mountains?

PREVIEW

What's So Good about Mountains?

In this *informational text*, the author explains why mountains are important for people and animals. An informational text gives information and presents facts. You can find informational texts in books, magazines, and on the Internet. As you read, look for causes and effects to help you understand why mountains are important.

Earth Science

Read 3•03

What's So Good about Mountains?

Water!

When you're thirsty, you drink water. When you want to take a shower, you turn on a faucet. But did you ever think about where all the water comes from? One reason mountains are important is that they provide fresh water for over half of all the people in the world. That's about three-and-a-half billion people! Can you imagine how much water is used by all those people?

When the sun warms water in rivers and oceans, the liquid is transformed into water vapor that rises into the air. When enough water vapor cools, it condenses, and small drops of water are formed. The drops of water turn into clouds. In the clouds, small drops of water join to make larger drops. When those drops become too heavy, they are released as rain or snow. Some rain soaks into the ground, and some of the rain runs over the ground into streams, rivers, lakes, and the ocean. This process is called the water cycle.

Mountains can affect the water cycle. The size and shape of a mountain pushes the water vapor up toward the mountaintop. When water drops fall on mountains, most of the water is stored as snow and as ice in glaciers. When the snow melts in the spring, the water flows down the slopes into streams, waterfalls, and rivers. Mountains are effective at storing water and are sometimes called the "water towers" of the world.

All of the big rivers on Earth start in the mountains. For example, in India, the Ganges River starts in the Himalayan mountain range and flows for 2,500 kilometers into the Bay of Bengal and the Indian Ocean. Another example is the Rio Grande, which begins in the Rocky Mountains in the United States and flows all the way down to the Gulf of Mexico.

Think
Why does rain fall? What happens before rain falls?

Animals!

Mountains are also important because they provide homes to many animals that don't exist anywhere else on Earth. You can find mountain gorillas in the mountains of East Africa and special bears called spectacled bears in the Andes. There are also snow leopards in the Himalayas.

Mount Cameroon is a mountain that is also one of Africa's largest active volcanoes, rising to more than 4,000 meters at its peak. It has 210 different species of birds and 70 species of butterflies. Mountains are home to many amazing animals and birds. Unfortunately, some of these animals are becoming rare. This is happening because people are taking more land and using more resources, such as water and wood. They are building farms and roads in the mountains. This means animals have less space to make their homes and find food.

Think

Why are some mountain animals becoming rare?

Food!

Did you know that 80 percent of the food we eat comes from just 20 types of plants? Six of these plants are found in the mountains! Do you like French fries? Well, guess what? Potatoes first came from the Andes, the world's longest mountain range, which stretches 7,000 kilometers through South America. Today, farmers in the Andes grow 2,000 different types of potatoes.

In the mountains of Nepal, about 2,000 different types of rice are farmed. Corn is found in the Sierra Mountains of Mexico. And the best quality tea and coffee are grown at an altitude of about 1,500 meters. Farmers sometimes build terraces into steep mountainsides and hills to grow crops and help control the flow of water. The terraces made by Inca Indians 500 years ago are still used by farmers in the Andes Mountains in Peru.

Remember how water from rain and snow flows down mountains? With rich soil and a lot of water, mountain valleys are often good places to grow fruits, vegetables, and other crops.

Think

Why do farmers grow plants in the mountains?

Understand

Comprehension

Think Talk with your partner about three things you learned in "What's So Good about Mountains?"

A **Fill in the organizer with causes and effects from the text on pages 112–113.**

Cause (why something happens)	Effect (what happens)
______________________	______________________
______________________	______________________
______________________	______________________
______________________	______________________
______________________	______________________

B **Circle the correct answer.**

1 In the mountains, where is the water?

a in the trees
b in snow
c in rocks
d in a tower

2 How many species of birds are there on Mount Cameroon?

a 70
b 2,000
c 210
d 4,000

3 What grows in the mountains?

a oranges
b palm trees
c seaweed
d potatoes

4 Why are mountains important?

a animals
b food
c water
d all of the above

C **Words in Context** **Look again at the words you circled in the text. Write them in the correct sentences.**

1 The river Thames ______________ through London.
2 Computers are great for ______________ big files like videos and photos.
3 Oil and coal are mineral ______________.
4 The cloud ______________ water as rain and snow.
5 The old school has been ______________ into a community center.
6 When water ______________, clouds get heavy and it rains.

Grammar in Use

D **Listen and read along. Then circle True (T) or False (F).** 3•04

People call mountains water towers. Mountains are called water towers.

These sentences mean the same thing. T F

E **Learn Grammar** Passive

We can say the same thing in two different ways by making active or **passive** sentences. Using the passive is a good idea if you don't know exactly who or what does something.

Active	Passive
People **find** corn in the mountains.	Corn **is found** in the mountains.
Do people **grow** rice in Canada?	**Is** rice **grown** in Canada?

Change the sentences to the passive. Write the missing word.

1 People eat potatoes all over the world. Potatoes are __________ all over the world.

2 Mr. Bezana grows the strawberries in a greenhouse. The strawberries are __________ in a greenhouse.

3 Do people climb mountains in South America? Are mountains __________ in South America?

F **Choose three sentences below and rewrite them in the passive. Then say them to your partner.**

People eat pizza in many countries.	Do people grow apples in Korea?
Farmers grow corn in the Andes.	People make French fries from potatoes.
People don't grow rice in England.	

Communicate

Listening

Think **Do you think the weather is the same on all of the mountains in the world?**

A **Learn** Listening for Key Words

Sometimes you need to listen for key information. For example, you may need to fill out a form or a chart. Look at **B**. Read the chart before you listen, and identify any key words that you might need to listen for.

Listen. What is the woman talking about? Check (✓) the correct box. 3•05

weather ☐ sports ☐ people ☐

B **Listen again and complete the chart.** 3•06

Location	Plants	Animals	Weather
peak of the mountain	no plants	no ________	very ________
high up the mountain	some ________ plants	a few ________	cold, ________, and windy.
near the bottom of the mountain	many ________ and trees	________ animals	warm with some snow in ________

Speaking 3•07

C **Take turns interviewing each other about living in the mountains.**

- **top of the mountain**
- **bottom of the mountain**
- **activities**
- **weather**

Word Study

D **Learn** Prefixes *in-* and *im-*

Remember: A prefix is added to the beginning of words to make new words. The prefixes in- and im- make the new words negative.

I don't like to wait. I'm impatient.
Exercise! You shouldn't be inactive.

Listen and say the words. Write the words by adding *in-* or *im-*. Write sentences in your notebook with the words you made by adding prefixes. 3·08 A-Z

1	correct	______	5	patient	______
2	possible	______	6	direct	______
3	perfect	______	7	expensive	______
4	active	______	8	polite	______

Writing Study

E **Learn** Colons

To add a list to an independent clause, use a colon (:) before your list.

We bought food for the party: cake, ice cream, chips, and fruit.

Complete these sentences with your own lists. Use a colon and include at least three things.

1 I like to play these sports ______________________________.

2 I saw these animals on TV ______________________________.

3 I like to do these activities for fun ______________________________.

Write Now practice writing in the **Workbook**. page 109

BIG QUESTION 6

Why are mountains important?

Mountains are important because they provide fresh water.

What are some other ways that mountains are important?

UNIT 12 Get Ready

Words

A **Listen and say the words. Then read and listen to the sentences.** 3•09

endless	stammer	awestruck	jagged	pointy	miniature
stern	arch	mutter	squirm	scowl	stretch

1 The mountain is so big, it looks **endless**.
2 I **stammered** when I spoke, because I was so nervous.
3 The view was so impressive that we felt **awestruck**.
4 The **jagged** rocks were uneven and looked sharp.
5 I have some very **pointy** shoes. They look funny.
6 Look! It's a **miniature** tree. It's much smaller than a normal one.
7 My teacher looked very **stern** when I forgot my homework.
8 There is a curved **arch** over the doorway.
9 I can't hear what you're saying when you **mutter**.
10 Nick **squirmed** in his seat because it was uncomfortable.
11 You look angry when you **scowl**!
12 I need to **stretch**. I've been sitting down a long time.

B **Circle the one that doesn't belong.**

1	tiny	huge	miniature	very small
2	stern	serious	cheerful	severe
3	smile	frown	look unhappy	scowl
4	infinite	endless	continuous	limited
5	mutter	listen	talk quietly	whisper
6	sharp	pointy	rounded	peaked

C **Choose the best word to complete each sentence.**

1 The rocks at the peak of the mountain are ______________.
2 At the lake, we were often ______________ by the beauty of the sunsets.
3 Cats like to take naps. When they wake up, they need to ______________.
4 There is a big stone ______________ at the entrance to the library.
5 Don't ______________ in your seat. Please sit still.

squirm
awestruck
stretch
jagged
arch

Before You Read

Think What sort of person would be a good explorer? Discuss the answer with your partner.

D **Learn** The Five Ws

When you read a story, think about the **five Ws** (**who**, **what**, **where**, **when**, and **why**). You can use a chart like the one below to help you follow the story.

Read the story. Then fill in the chart.

A Race for Mom

Ana just needed to lace up her sneakers and then she and her older brother would leave for the stadium. She couldn't believe the day had finally arrived. It was a cold morning, but Ana wasn't going to let that bother her. She'd been cold before. At 8:00 a.m., she was going to run in her very first marathon. Her mother wouldn't be there to see her cross the finish line, but that was exactly the point. Ana was running in memory of her mom. She smiled just thinking of how proud her mom would have been.

Who? ____________________

What? ____________________

____

Where? ____________________

When? ____________________

Why? ____________________

____

E **Words in Context** Scan the story on pages 120–121 and circle these words. As you read, try to guess what the words mean.

silhouette **shielded** **teasing** **folded** **embarrassed** **distant**

F Now turn to pages 120–121. Read the title and look at the pictures. What do you think the story is about?

PREVIEW

The Lost Explorer

In this story, you'll read about a boy and a girl who meet an old man in the mountains. This story is a *fictional narrative*, which means it was invented by an author. The story didn't happen in real life. A fictional narrative has characters, a plot, and a setting. As you read, think about the five Ws.

Susannah Appelbaum is the author of the critically acclaimed children's series *The Poisons of Caux*. She comes from a long line of doctors and philosophers, but alas, no explorers.

Read 3•10

The Lost Explorer

"Listen, a waterfall!" Samantha said.

Her brother Robert listened. There was the tinkling, musical sound of water from somewhere up the path. The dark silhouette of Entwhistle Peak, a jagged mountain in the Andes range, towered above them against the sky.

Samantha looked for her parents, who were picnicking in the field below, and then dashed off after Robert. They stopped beside an outcrop of pointy rocks and a beautiful deep pool. From high above, a thin stream of water tumbled, catching the light.

"It's so beautiful here," Samantha sighed.

Robert shielded his eyes, scanning the sky. Miniature birds circled the summit of the mountain.

"There's an old stone tower up there," Robert said. "I bet it's Sir Geoffrey Entwhistle's secret fort."

Samantha knew the mountain was named for the famous explorer, but she also had read her nature guide back at the lodge.

"It's hardly a secret on top of the mountain," Samantha said, teasing. "Besides, it's an old weather station."

"We'll see about that," Robert muttered.

"Wait!" she called, but he was gone.

The thin path disappeared around a rocky bend, and when Samantha finally scrambled up, her brother was nowhere to be seen. The open sky was slate gray and filled with clouds; a storm was rolling in. Behind her, the descent to the valley was very steep.

Think
Which of the five Ws can you answer?

My brother and his crazy ideas, she thought.

A stick snapped and Samantha jumped. Robert was bounding out from beneath some trees. She scowled at her brother and folded her arms across her chest. "You scared me!"

"I told you it was his secret fort!" Robert said, pointing.

A set of stone stairs was carved into the side of the mountain beneath a gated arch. The steps twisted around the peak.

"This is it!" he called over his shoulder. Samantha scrambled after him, and they emerged before a stern-looking tower. "The explorer's hiding place!" Robert said, triumphant.

"The weather station," Samantha corrected.

As she spoke, the tower door swung open, and a kind-looking old man stood in the doorway.

"Hello there," the man said. "It's not often I get visitors."

"Who—who are you?" Robert stammered.

"I am a scientist. The mountain is a great place to observe nature and weather patterns. For over twenty years, the weather forecasts that were shown on TV were mine." He smiled at the pair. "And who are you?"

"I am Samantha," she said. "And this is my brother Robert."

Robert scowled; his face was flushed and embarrassed.

"Don't mind him. He thought you were a lost explorer. Sir Geoffrey Entwhistle."

"Lost, is he? He must not be a very good explorer," the old man said. "Well, Samantha and Robert, come in for a cup of hot cocoa. The storm will clear soon."

Inside there was a crackling fire, and shelves held old books and strange metal objects.

"I have the best job in the world," the old man said. "This mountain is not only a scientific outpost, it is a place of great beauty. I've been here for many years."

Just then, the sun peeked out from behind the storm clouds. The view was breathtaking; the mountain range stretched out in all directions and the sky was reflected in a distant lake. Samantha and Robert marveled at the sight.

"I'll show you the way home," the old man said, opening the door. "If you trust me to not get lost." He winked at Robert.

"Wait," Samantha said. "We haven't learned your name!"

"Ah," he said. "My friends call me Geoffrey."

Think
Which of the five Ws can you answer?

Understand

Comprehension

Think Talk with your partner about the characters in the story. Who was your favorite character in "The Lost Explorer"? What did you think about where the story was set?

A Re-read the story and fill in the chart. Then compare answers with your partner.

Who? ______________________________
What? ______________________________
____
Where? ______________________________
When? ______________________________
Why? ______________________________
____

B Circle the correct answer.

1 Geoffrey Entwhistle had a secret ______
- **a** castle.
- **b** hiding place.
- **c** fort.
- **d** treehouse.

2 Samantha and Robert's parents were ______
- **a** at the hotel.
- **b** having a picnic.
- **c** visiting relatives.
- **d** home.

3 Mr. Entwhistle is a ______
- **a** scientist.
- **b** doctor.
- **c** writer.
- **d** teacher.

4 Robert's face flushed when Samantha introduced him because ______
- **a** he was afraid.
- **b** he was hungry.
- **c** he was crying.
- **d** he was embarrassed.

C **Words in Context** Look again at the words you circled in the story. Write them in the correct sentences.

1 Joey ______________ his arms and looked angry.

2 I was very ______________ when I broke the window with my ball.

3 It's dark, but I can see a ______________ of a person through the window.

4 The sun was too bright, so I ______________ my eyes.

5 We heard a ______________ noise that sounded like an animal.

6 Please stop ______________ your little sister. It's not nice.

Workbook Grammar
pages 114–115

Grammar in Use

D **Listen and read along. Then circle True (T) or False (F).** 3•11

Mount Everest was climbed in 1953.
Sir Edmund Hillary and Tenzing Norgay climbed Mount Everest in 1953.
These sentences mean the same thing. T F

E **Learn Grammar** Past Passive

Remember: You can use the active or the passive to say the same thing in two different ways. You can also do this in the past tense.

Active	Passive
Someone **broke** my mom's favorite vase.	My mom's favorite vase **was broken**.
Someone **showed** the weather forecasts on TV.	The weather forecasts **were shown** on TV.

Read the story. Circle all the verbs you can find.

Last year, people organized a big party in my town. People put up decorations. People cooked food and played music. Children played games. Adults gave children gifts. People ate a lot of candy and cakes. Restaurants prepared ice cream and sodas. People lit fireworks! It was a fantastic party!

F **Work with your partner. Take turns re-telling the story using the passive.**

Communicate

Listening

Think Do you listen to or watch weather reports? How can a weather report help you plan your day?

A Listen. Who is speaking? 3•12

B Listen again and circle the correct answer. 3•13

1 In the early morning, it will be **cloudy and breezy / sunny and calm.**

2 By noon, people will be able to **go skiing / go hiking.**

3 Hikers should take **a sweater / an umbrella.**

4 After 4:00 p.m., hikers should **go home / keep hiking.**

5 On the upper slopes, there will be **fog and heavy rain / clouds and sunshine.**

Speaking 3•14

C **Learn** Asking for Advice

You can ask someone to give you advice by using Do you think ...? and Would it be a good idea to ...?

Do you think **I should go hiking today?** Would it be a good idea to **take some climbing equipment?**

Work with your partner. Take turns asking and giving advice about these situations.

- **You are going to the beach on a very hot day.**
- **You are going to the mountains on a cold and snowy day.**

Word Study

D **Learn** More Synonyms

Remember: Synonyms are words that mean almost the same thing. They help you write in a more interesting way.

The room was large. He had never seen such a big room.

Listen and say the words. Match each word with its synonym. Work with your partner to write sentences for four words and their synonyms. 3•15 A-Z

1 shine	**2** ill	**3** frightened	**4** clever	**5** gigantic	**6** weird	**7** cautious	**8** swift
a sick	**b** afraid	**c** careful	**d** smart	**e** huge	**f** sparkle	**g** quick	**h** strange

Writing Study

E **Learn** Irregular Past Participles

Remember: Some verbs in the past tense are irregular.
They have irregular past participles.

Present	Past	Past Participle
choose	**chose**	**chosen**
fly	**flew**	**flown**

He chose to go out in the snowstorm.
The birds have flown away.

Circle the correct verb form.

1 He **break / broke / broken** through the ice with a big stick.

2 A book was **written / wrote / write** about the mountain climber.

3 After many years, the name of the explorer was **knew / know / known**.

4 Robert **give / given / gave** Samantha a path to follow.

5 The climber broke his leg. He was **took / taken / take** to the hospital.

Write Now practice writing in the **Workbook**. page 117

Writing

A Read this story.

MOUNTAIN HIKE

When — It was a **cold January afternoon**
Who — and **Silvia and Marco** were scared.
Where and why — They'd left home early that morning to go for a long hike in **the mountains**. They'd walked several kilometers uphill in beautiful sunshine, and on the way, they'd seen gazelles, rabbits, and hawks. At lunchtime, they'd stopped by a clear mountain stream to eat their sandwiches and play a game of ball. But now, in the late afternoon, clouds were appearing over the peaks and rain was beginning to fall. To their surprise, the sky became very dark, almost as dark as night. Silvia and Marco realized they were lost.

Suddenly, a loud noise far away made both children jump. Snow was sliding off a peak of the mountain, causing an avalanche. Silvia and
Why — Marco knew that **avalanches were very dangerous**. People
What — sometimes got trapped in the falling snow. The children began to **run back down the mountainside** to safety, as fast as their legs would carry them. Luckily, the avalanche was much higher up the mountain. In the distance, they could see the bright, welcoming lights of their hometown, so they ran faster and faster, hoping that the sun would soon come out from behind a cloud to light their way.

B Answer the questions.

1 Where does the story take place?
2 Who are the characters?
3 When is the story happening?
4 Why are Silvia and Marco on the mountain?
5 What do the children do?

C Learn Writing a Story

Remember to give details to answer these questions when you write a story.

- **Characters:** Who will be in your story? What are their names? How do they know each other?
- **Setting:** Where and when does the story take place?
- **Problem:** What happens in the story? What problem do the characters have?
- **Solution:** How is the problem solved? How does the story end?

Write Now go to the **Workbook** to plan and write your own story. page 119

D Practice presenting your story. Then share your story with the class.

1 Practice reading your story aloud.
2 Decide where you can add gestures to the important parts of your story.
3 Practice using expression in your voice.
4 Read your story to the class.
5 Have fun! If you're having fun, the class will, too!
6 Ask your classmates what they like about your story.
7 After everyone has read their story, talk about the stories that you enjoyed.

BIG QUESTION 6

Why are mountains important?

A Watch the video. How are the mountains you see important?

B What are some answers to the Big Question? Talk about them with your partner.

C Complete the **Big Question Chart**. Then discuss it with the class.

Testing Practice 2

Reading and Writing

A **Read the article. Are sentences 1–5 right (a) or wrong (b)? If there is not enough information to answer *right* (a) or *wrong* (b), choose *doesn't say* (c). Circle your answer.**

Sometimes, people and animals behave in similar ways. Most animals and people will fight to defend their young. Animals and humans will collaborate with members of their own species to find food or shelter. When it comes to expressing ourselves, humans use speech, sound, and body movement. Animals aren't much different; they use sound and body movements, too. However, humans don't always succeed in communicating with each other, and neither do animals!

1 Animals are better than humans at collaborating to find food and shelter.
a right **b** wrong **c** doesn't say

2 Humans and animals communicate in very different ways.
a right **b** wrong **c** doesn't say

3 Humans often use computers to communicate with members of their own species.
a right **b** wrong **c** doesn't say

4 Animals sometimes use body movement to communicate.
a right **b** wrong **c** doesn't say

5 Members of the human species will fight to defend their children.
a right **b** wrong **c** doesn't say

B **Write a postcard in your notebook. Invite your friend Charles to come to an amusement park with you. Write 25–30 words.**

You might include:
- **where and when to meet**
- **what Charles should bring**
- **who else is coming**
- **what you plan to do there**

Tip
Use transition words to organize your writing (*first*, *then*, *next*, and *finally*).

Listening

C You will hear a short conversation. You will hear the conversation twice. After the conversation, match the pictures and words. 3•16

Tip
Before listening to the conversation, look at the pictures and read the words.

1 

2 

3 

4 

- **a** ice cream
- **b** almond milk
- **c** hot chocolate
- **d** chocolate bar

- **e** creamy
- **f** nutty
- **g** great
- **h** spicy
- **i** crunchy
- **j** delicious
- **k** smooth

Speaking

Part 1 Work with a partner. Ask and answer questions about your daily life.

1 What time do you usually get up in the morning?
2 What time do you usually leave your house for school in the morning?
3 How do you get to school?
4 What are your favorite foods to have for lunch?
5 What do you usually do after school?
6 What time do you go to bed on school nights?

Part 2 Your teacher will give you a sheet of paper with some information on it. One of you will get questions and one of you will get answers. Ask and answer with your partner.

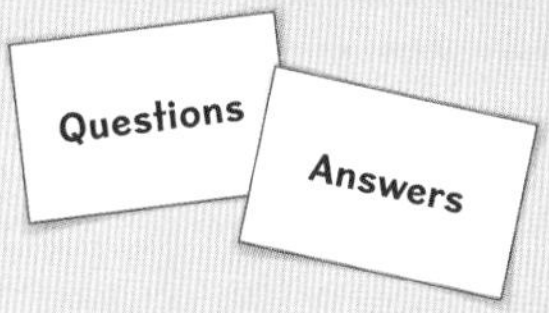

In units **13** and **14** you will:

WATCH a video about money.

LEARN about how money is used.

READ a folktale and an article about the history of money.

WRITE a summary.

PRESENT your summary to the class.

BIG QUESTION 7

Why do we use money?

A Watch the video. Then talk about it with your partner.

B Look at the picture and discuss it with your class.

1 Why are there different kinds of money?
2 Why do we have money?

C Think and answer the questions.

1 What is money?
2 What do you use money for?
3 What can people do with money?
4 What is the money in your country called?

D Discuss this topic with your class. Fill out the **Big Question Chart**.

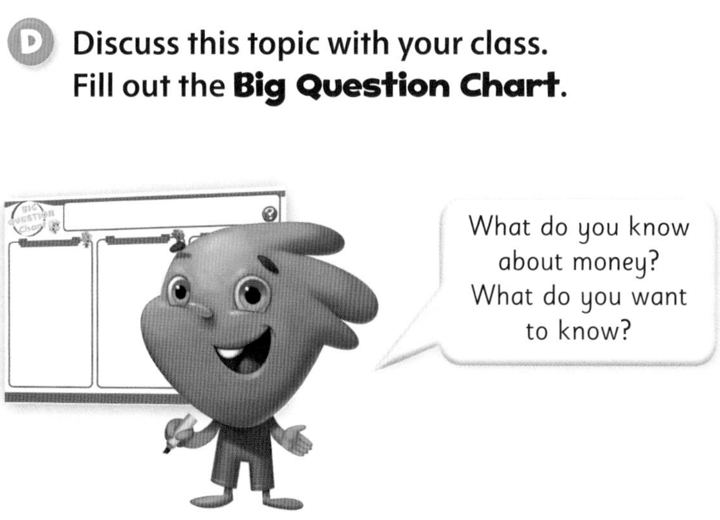

UNIT 13 Get Ready

Words

A Listen and say the words. Then read and listen to the sentences. 3•17

terrifying | nervously | rudely | politely | fierce | aggressively

delicate | bravely | greedy | shyly | wise | calmly

1 The big thunderstorm last night was **terrifying**.
2 "What have I done wrong?" I asked **nervously**.
3 "Go away!" the boy shouted **rudely**.
4 "May I help you?" the waiter asked **politely**.
5 The lion looked very **fierce** with its huge teeth and claws.
6 People sometimes behave **aggressively**. They attack others.
7 Vases are very **delicate**. They can break easily.
8 The firefighters **bravely** went into the burning house.
9 **Greedy** people always want more of everything.
10 He smiled at me **shyly** because he didn't know me.
11 **Wise** people make good decisions.
12 Tom reacted **calmly** to the bad news. He wasn't upset.

B Match. Then write another answer to each question.

1 What word describes a shy person? •	• bear
2 What things are delicate? •	• thunderstorm
3 What weather can be fierce? •	• quiet
4 What animal is terrifying? •	• taking a test
5 What makes students feel nervous? •	• flowers

C Which words have a positive meaning? Which are negative? Complete the chart.

rudely politely greedy calmly aggressively bravely wise

Positive	Negative

Before You Read

Think Answer the questions.

1 What is a thief?

2 What kinds of things do thieves steal?

D **Learn** Summarizing

Summarizing means re-telling the most important parts of a story or an article. Imagine that you're going to tell a friend what you've read. What is the text about? What are the important events?

Use a chart like the one below to help you summarize.

Re-read "Choco Choco Boom Boom!" on pages 100–101. Write the important events from the story in the chart. Then complete the sentences to summarize the story.

Title: ________________________

Main character: ________________________

Main idea: ________________________

Important event: ________________________

Important event: ________________________

Important event: ________________________

A girl named ________ visits ____________ and wants to taste the best ____________. She finds a __________ where the shopkeeper gives her a special __________. When she eats half of the chocolate, she feels dizzy. She opens her eyes to see that she's in a __________ where a man is making chocolates. He is ____________________, the inventor of the praline. He teaches her how to make ____________, and then it's time to go. Akiko eats the other half of the praline and ends up back in the store in Brussels.

E **Words in Context** **Scan the story on pages 134–135 and circle these words. As you read, try to guess what the words mean.**

muscles **growling** **stirring** **mouth-watering** **tempting** **staring**

F **Look at the pictures on pages 134–135. Which character do you think is rude and aggressive? How do you know?**

PREVIEW

The Sound of Money and the Smell of Soup

This story is a Turkish *folktale* about a boy who is accused of stealing something. Folktales are stories that have been passed down through generations. They usually contain a valuable lesson that the reader can learn from. As you read, think about the setting, the characters, the problem, and the solution. This will help you summarize the story.

Read 3·18

The *Sound of Money*

Many more years ago than anyone can remember, there was a young man named Erman who lived in a village in the Kingdom of Atinka, a country far away from everywhere.

Erman had little money. In fact, he only had three gold coins. One day, Erman went on a journey to find a job. He traveled over land and sea, through deserts and forests, across rivers and mountains, until he arrived in a city. As he looked around, he was fascinated by the sights, sounds, and smells of the market. There were people selling jewels, spices, leather, and clothes. There were donkeys, sheep, goats, and camels. There were musicians banging drums and playing flutes. Surely here Erman would find a job!

Erman saw a sign: ROOM TO RENT. Very nervously, he knocked at the door. A terrifying man with huge muscles opened it.

"What do you want?" the man hollered rudely.

"A room, please, sir," answered Erman politely.

"Three gold coins!" replied the man. He looked fierce. Erman began to shake.

"But, but …," said Erman.

"Three gold coins!" repeated the man aggressively. Erman had no choice. Handing the man the only three coins he had, he went up to his room.

The next morning, Erman woke up early. He was starving! What was that delicious smell? It was a delicate mixture of chicken, carrots, spices, herbs, and garlic. Erman's stomach made a growling noise like a tiger. He galloped down the staircase, following the smell with his nose in the air.

In the kitchen, the rude man was stirring a pot of soup as big as a bathtub with a wooden spoon. Several people were waiting to pay for their lunches. Erman

Think
What is the setting for the story? Who are the characters so far?

and the Smell of Soup

turned to the man bravely and said: “May I have some of that mouth-watering soup?”

“Three gold coins,” yelled the man threateningly.

“But, but …,” said Erman. He didn’t have any gold coins left, so he went back up to his room. He pulled a chair onto his balcony. From there, he could smell the soup with all its tempting flavors.

Sniff, sniff, sniff. Erman sucked in the air and imagined he was eating the greedy man’s soup.

“What are you doing?” yelled the man. He was standing on the street staring up at Erman.

“Nothing,” said Erman shyly. “I was just smelling your delicious soup.”

“You are a thief!” screamed the man. “You have stolen my smells! I will take you to court and make you pay for the smell of my soup!”

He dragged Erman down the staircase, along the street, and straight into the law court.

In the court, the Hodja, who was a wise man and a judge, was reading a newspaper. Everybody asked him to decide who was right and who was wrong. That was the Hodja’s job. The Hodja looked at Erman, and then he looked at the terrifying man.

“What’s the problem?” he asked.

“This boy has stolen my smells!” screamed the man. His face was purple with anger.

“And you want to be paid for the smells?” asked the Hodja.

“Yes, I do!” bellowed the man.

“Then I will pay you,” said the Hodja calmly. He took three gold coins from his pocket and, one by one, he threw them into a metal bowl.

Think
What is the problem?

“There you are,” said the Hodja, returning to his newspaper. “You can leave now.”

“But … but … where’s my money?” cried the man.

The Hodja looked at the man over the top of his newspaper.

“I have paid you for the smell of soup with the sound of money,” the Hodja said fiercely. “Now, go away!”

Comprehension

Think In your opinion, who was right in the story? Was it the Hodja or the soup maker? Talk about it with your partner.

A Fill in the chart with information from the story. Then write a summary of the story in your notebook.

Title: ______________________________
Main character: ______________________________
Main idea: ______________________________
____
Important event: ______________________________
____
Important event: ______________________________
____
Important event: ______________________________
____

B Write answers to the questions in your notebook. Discuss them with your class.

1 Why did Erman leave his home in the Kingdom of Atinka?
2 What did the rude man think Erman was stealing?
3 Did Erman think he was stealing?
4 How did the Hodja solve the problem?
5 What lesson can we learn from this folktale?

C **Words in Context** Look again at the words you circled in the story. Then write them in the correct sentences.

1 A man with huge ______________ lifted the giant weight.
2 The hungry wolf was ______________ loudly somewhere in the forest.
3 Please stop ______________ at me. It's impolite.
4 The cook took a large spoon and began ______________ a big pot on the stove.
5 The smell of the delicious cookies was ______________ .
6 Jen was so hungry that just the thought of a delicious meal was ______________ .

Workbook Grammar
pages 126–127

Grammar in Use

D **Listen and read along. Then circle the correct answer.** 3•19

Which sentence tells you more about the soup?

a He cooked some soup. **b** He cooked some delicious soup.

E **Learn Grammar** Adjectives and Adverbs

Remember: **Adjectives** tell you more about nouns.

A terrifying man with huge muscles opened the door.

Adverbs tell you more about verbs. An adverb of manner tells you how something happens.

"Three gold coins!" repeated the man aggressively.

An adverb of frequency tells you how often something happens.

The Hodja was reading a newspaper, as he often did.

Use the adjectives and adverbs in the box to improve the sentences.

hungrily	nervously	quickly	often

1 I ran ______________ up the stairs.
2 "What's for dinner?" asked Sam ______________.
3 Police officers ______________ chase thieves.
4 "Are you OK?" the man asked ______________.

F **Think of sentences for each word and say them to your partner.**

beautiful	sometimes	greedily
noisily	fierce	always

Communicate

Listening

Think Do you save money? Do you think it's easier to spend money or save it?

A **Listen to the conversation. Circle True (T) or False (F).** 3•20

1 The money bank has five separate slots. T F

2 The money bank is transparent. You can see the money in it. T F

3 Saving money is for things you want to buy in many years' time. T F

4 Investing money is for things you want to buy in many years' time. T F

5 You cannot get your money out of the money bank. T F

6 *Donating* means the same as *giving*. T F

B **Listen again. What is the difference between saving and investing money? What would you donate money to? Discuss your answers with the class.** 3•21

Speaking 3•22

C **Learn** Future Plans

Use want to and need to when talking about future plans.

I want to save money for a new soccer ball.

I need to save money for a new backpack.

Ask and answer with your partner about the topics below.

Things I want now:
- game
- magazine
- sneakers
- T-shirt

Things I need later:
- education
- computer
- home
- car

Word Study

D **Learn** Phrasal Verbs

Some verbs are used with prepositions such as **across**, **down**, **for**, **in**, **off**, **out**, **up**, and **with**. These two-part verbs are called **phrasal verbs**. The word that comes after the verb changes the meaning.

Phrasal Verb	Meaning	Example
break down	stop working	**The car broke down on the road.**
break into	enter a building by force	**A man broke into our house.**
break off	remove a part of something	**Break off a piece of chocolate for me.**

Listen, say, and number the words. Then work with your partner to use each phrasal verb in a sentence. 3•23 A-Z

____ hand in	____ take off	____ break down	____ break into
____ put on	____ take out	____ stand up	____ break off

Writing Study

E **Learn** Adverbs of Degree

Some adverbs make adjectives and other adverbs stronger. These are called **adverbs of degree**. They include **very**, **really**, **absolutely**, and **extremely**.

Pia finished her work extremely quickly. (extremely = adverb; quickly = adverb)

These noodles are absolutely delicious! (absolutely = adverb; delicious = adjective)

Choose an adverb from the box above to complete each sentence.

1 That singer is ______________ good.
2 The driver drove ______________ fast.
3 You are ______________ right!
4 You make cakes ______________ well.

Now practice writing in the **Workbook**. page 129

BIG QUESTION 7

Why do we use money?

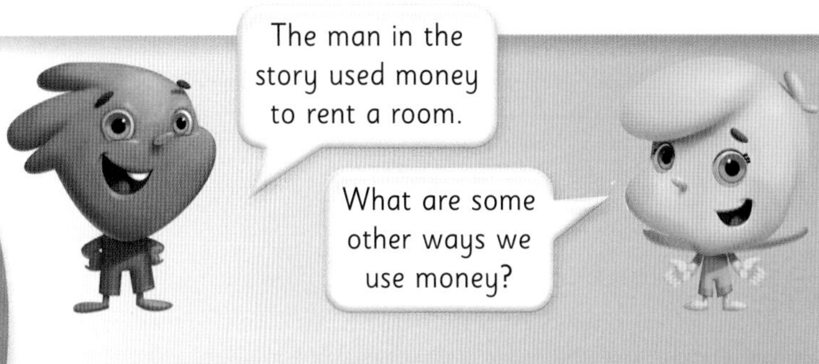

UNIT 14 Get Ready

Words

A Listen and say the words. Then read and listen to the sentences. 3•24

bank	currency	coins	barter	copy	bill
spend	pay	borrow	exchange	owe	lend

1 People save money by putting it in a **bank**.
2 **Currency** is the system of money that a country uses.
3 I counted all my **coins**, and I had enough to buy a candy bar.
4 When people **barter**, they exchange goods without money.
5 You can **copy** an essay or a drawing on a photocopier.
6 How many **bills** are there in your wallet?
7 I don't want to **spend** too much money. I like to save it.
8 Let's **pay** for our milkshakes. How much do they cost?
9 Can I **borrow** some money from you? I don't have enough.
10 I'd like to **exchange** this T-shirt for a different one. It's too big.
11 How much do I **owe** you for the book you bought for me?
12 Can you **lend** me a little bit of money?

B Look at how the words are used above. Then write them in the correct category.

Things You Can See	
______	______
______	______
______	______
______	______
______	______
______	______
______	______

Things You Can Do	
______	______
______	______
______	______
______	______
______	______
______	______
______	______

C Answer the questions as a class. Say as many of your ideas as you can.

1 What things do people pay for?
2 What's the difference between paying for something and borrowing something?
3 What things do you lend to your friends? What things do you borrow?

Before You Read

Think What have you learned about money so far?

D **Learn** Compare and Contrast

When you read, try to **compare and contrast** the information. Comparing means thinking about ideas that are alike. Contrasting means thinking about ideas that are different.

Read the text. How are the games different? How are they alike? Fill in the diagram.

Video Games: Which Should You Buy?

There are two new games available this month. *Escape!* is an adventure game set in a castle. *Supercool!* is a mystery game set in a jungle. Both games cost $9.99, and both can be played on a computer.

Both games have simple instructions and are very easy to play. However, *Escape!* has five levels of difficulty, and *Supercool!* has only three. For more challenge, buy *Escape!*

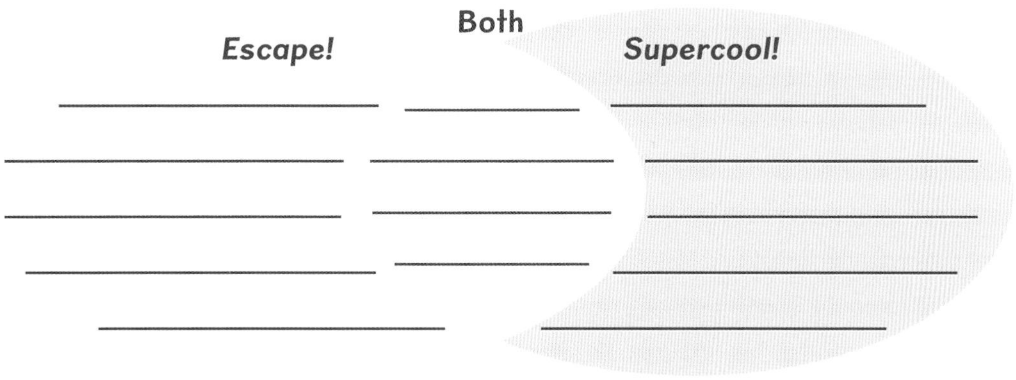

E **Words in Context** Scan the article on pages 142–143 and circle these words. As you read, try to guess what the words mean.

crops **shells** **valuable** **silver** **print** **portraits**

F Look at the article on pages 142–143. Where do you think this text comes from? How do you know? Share your ideas with the class.

PREVIEW

The History of Money

In this *website article*, you'll learn about the history of money and different forms of money. A website can provide a lot of information about a topic. It often has links that you can click on to find out more. As you read, compare and contrast the information.

Social Studies: History

Elizabeth Cody Kimmel is an author of over 30 books for children. Her books have been translated and published in countries across the globe.

THE HISTORY OF MONEY

When Did It All Start?

Between 11,000 and 6,000 years ago (no one is completely sure when), people started exchanging cows, sheep, camels, and crops to get the things they needed. This is called bartering. People barter one thing for another thing. Here's how it worked in the beginning:

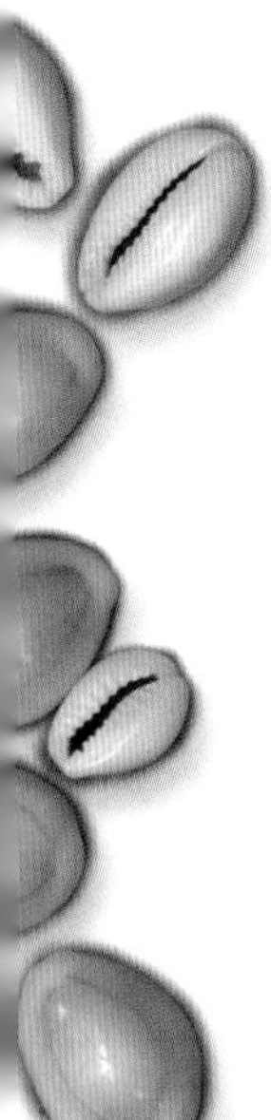

From Shells and Feathers to Coins

▲ Before coins, people used feathers or seashells as money.

Around 3,000 years ago, people decided that shells were a good form of money. But why? The answer is simple. Shells are beautiful, they're hard, and they don't break easily, so they last a long time. You can't find shells everywhere, and that makes them precious, so shells became valuable. If people wanted something, they would give shells for it. Other people did the same thing with feathers.

Next, about two hundred years later, the first coin was invented in China. The coins were made out of metal. Nowadays, we have small, round coins, but back then, they were made into different shapes in different countries.

Later, people used precious metals, like gold and silver, to make coins. In Lydia, which is now part of the country we call Turkey, a mixture of silver and gold was used to make coins. But guess what? Coins are heavy! If you had a lot of coins in your pocket all the time, they would make a hole!

◀ This is one of the earliest coins ever made.

Think

What has changed? Are ideas about money the same or different now?

Printed Money and Paper Money

About 1,200 years ago, the Chinese started to print money, but it wasn't paper money. They used leather from animals' skins. It wasn't until the seventh century that they decided to use paper. At last the world had its first paper currency. Paper is light and easy to carry. If you had paper money, you wouldn't need so many coins. Strangely enough, it took many more centuries for other countries around the world to start using paper money.

One of the problems with paper money was that it was easy to copy. Early banknotes, or bills, were printed in black and white. People who could draw well could easily copy them. Now bills are colorful. They have complicated designs, which are often pictures or portraits of people, and metal threads, long thin lines that go across the bill. That makes them very difficult for anyone to copy.

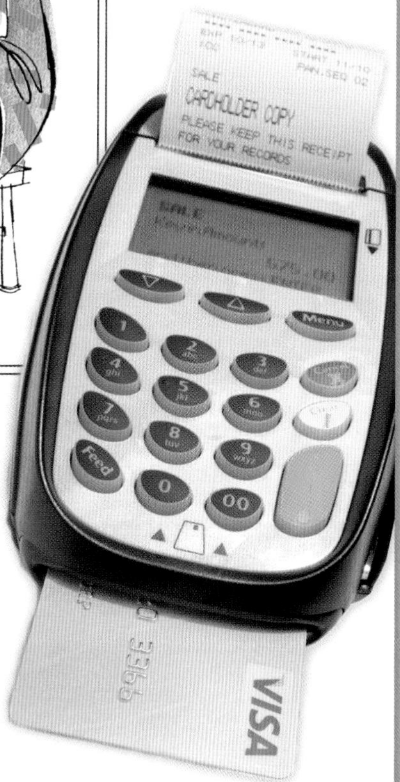

Invisible Money

We still have paper money and coins, but now we also pay for things electronically. Many people do their shopping online because now you can buy almost anything you want on the Internet. To pay electronically, we use plastic cards, including credit cards and debit cards. Using one of these cards tells the bank to pay another person, store, or restaurant for goods or services. We can borrow money from the bank this way, too. The bank lends us money for a certain amount of time, and we pay back what we owe them later. Maybe one day we won't need coins and bills at all!

Think

What has changed? How are ideas about money the same or different now?

Understand

Comprehension

Think Talk with your partner about three interesting facts from the website article. Were you surprised by the information?

A **Fill in the diagram using information from the website. Compare your diagram with your partner's.**

Paper Money — **Both** — **Invisible Money**

B **Write answers to the questions in your notebook. Then discuss them as a class.**

1 Before coins were invented, what two things did people use as currency?
2 What were the first coins made of?
3 Where did people mix silver and gold to make coins?
4 What did the Chinese use first to print their money on?
5 Why are banknotes colorful, and why do they have complicated designs?
6 What two types of cards can we use to pay for things electronically?

C **Words in Context** **Look again at the words you circled in the article. Then write them next to the correct descriptions.**

1 a precious metal ______________
2 worth money ______________
3 pictures of people ______________
4 to make an image with ink ______________
5 eggs have these ______________
6 plants that are grown for food ______________

Workbook Grammar pages 134–135

Grammar in Use

D **Listen and read along. Then circle Yes or No.** 3•26

Does Sonya have a plane? **Yes** **No**

E **Learn Grammar** Unreal Conditional

Use the **unreal conditional** to talk about things that aren't possible now.

If you had paper money, you wouldn't need so many coins.

Check (✓) the correct sentence in each pair.

1 ☐ If I have a bike, I would get to school quicker.
☐ If I had a bike, I would get to school quicker.

2 ☐ If my friend could fly a plane, we would go to the North Pole.
☐ If my friend could fly a plane, we will go to the North Pole.

3 ☐ If I won a prize, I would be very happy.
☐ If I win a prize, I would be very happy.

F **What would you do? Tell your partner.**

If I could drive a car ...
If I had some money ...
If I went to another country on vacation ...
If I didn't have to go to school next week ...
If I met someone famous ...

Communicate

Listening

Think **Why might people give their money away?**

A **Learn** Listening for Speakers

When you listen, listen carefully to identify the speakers. Ask yourself:

- Who is speaking first?
- Who is answering?
- How many people are speaking?

Listen to the conversation. How many people are speaking? 3•27

B **Listen again. Read the questions and check (✓) the correct answers.** 3•28

1 Who would buy something for someone else?
☐ Sami ☐ Ravi ☐ Satomi

2 Who would invest some money?
☐ Sami ☐ Ravi ☐ Satomi

3 Who would donate some money?
☐ Sami ☐ Ravi ☐ Satomi

4 What job is mentioned?
☐ lawyer ☐ teacher ☐ doctor

Speaking 3•29

C **You have 100 dollars to donate. Who will you help? Take turns asking and answering with your partner.**

- **hospital**
- **school**
- **children's charity**
- **animal clinic**

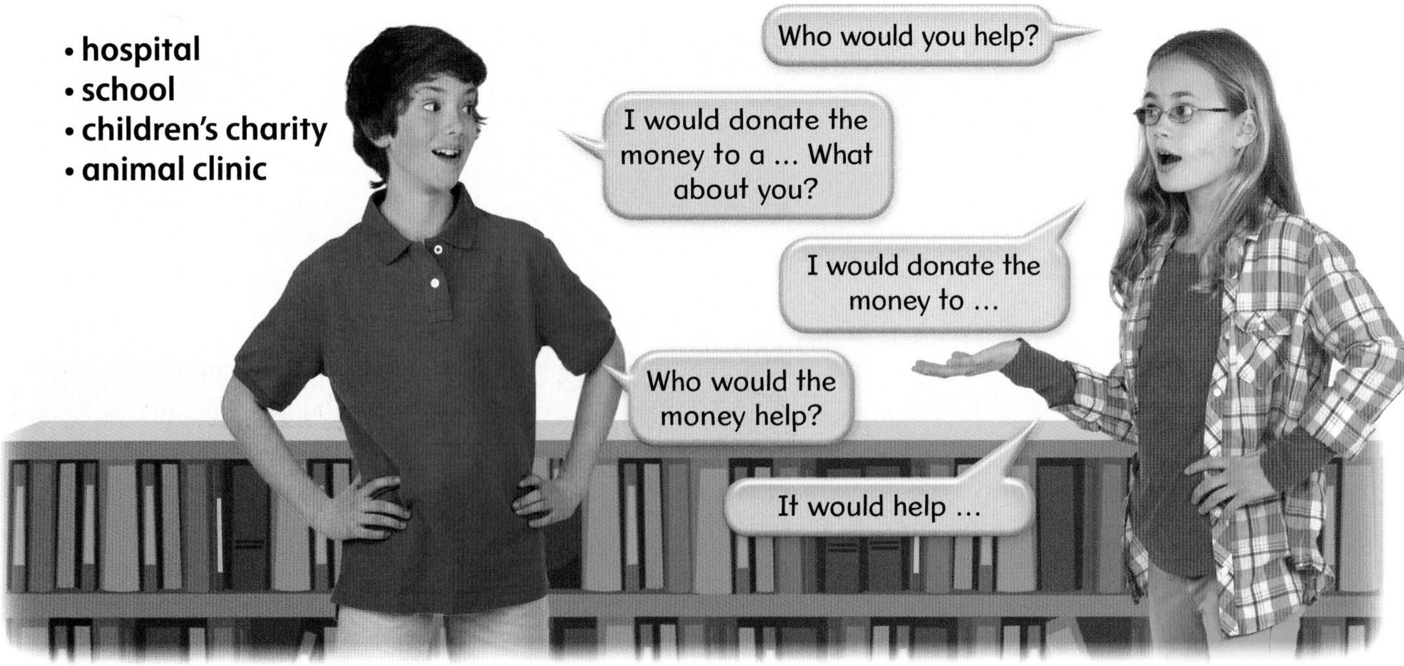

Word Study

D **Learn** Suffix *-ive*

The suffix -ive can be added to the end of some verbs.
It changes the verb into an adjective.

act + ive = active

create + ive = creative

Listen, say, and number the words. 3•30 A-Z

____ attractive	____ possessive	____ collaborative	____ active
____ decorative	____ protective	____ cooperative	____ creative

E **Work with your partner to write a paragraph using at least four of the adjectives above.**

Writing Study

F **Learn** Similes

You can make your writing more interesting by comparing things with as and like.

It's as cold as ice in here!
You're as brave as a lion!
My bedroom is like a nest, all cozy and warm.
My little brother eats very quickly, like a shark!

Finish these sentences with your own similes. Us *as … as* and *like*.

1 Our home is like ______________________________.

2 I'm as happy as ______________________________.

3 You're as talented ______________________________.

4 He plays the flute ______________________________.

5 The train took forever. The train ______________________________.

6 I ran quickly to catch the bus ______________________________.

Write Now practice writing in the **Workbook**. page 137

Wrap Up

Writing

A Read this summary of "Chatterboxes" from pages 80–81.

Title

Short introduction	Many animals communicate. They communicate for different reasons.
Most important details	Animals have certain reasons for communicating, including warning of danger. An example of this is a rabbit thumping its back legs. Some animals communicate to scare away predators. Others communicate to attract a mate, or to find food.
Short Examples	There are different types of animal communication: communication between animals of the same species (for example, monkeys communicating with each other), communication between animals of different species (for example, the honey badger and the honeyguide), and communication between animals and humans (for example, dolphins and people).
Short conclusion	Animals use a wide variety of sounds and movements to communicate.

B Answer the questions.

1 What does the writer put at the beginning of the summary?
2 Does the writer have an introduction?
3 What kind of details does the writer include?
4 Does the writer give short or long examples?
5 Does the writer use his or her own words or the author's words?

C Learn Writing a Summary

- Start your summary by telling the name of the article, story, or other text that you're summarizing.
- Include a short introduction. This should be about the main idea of the whole text.
- Include details from the text. Write only the most important things.
- Include very short examples if necessary.
- Remember to write the summary in your own words. Don't copy the author's words. Think about what you would tell a friend if they asked what the text was about.
- When you've finished your first draft, go back and read it again. Take out any information that is not absolutely necessary.

Write Now go to the **Workbook** to plan and write your own summary. page 139

D Present your summary.

1 Working in small groups, present your summaries to each other. Listen closely to each summary.

2 As a class, discuss the following questions:
- Why do you think each person's summary is slightly different?
- What makes some summaries more effective than others?
- How does writing a summary help you understand the reading better?

BIG QUESTION 7

Why do we use money?

A Watch the video. How do you see people using money?

B What are some answers to the Big Question? Talk about them with your partner.

C Complete the **Big Question Chart**. Then discuss it with the class.

In units **15** and **16** you will:

WATCH a video about self-expression.

LEARN about different art forms.

READ a play and learn about unusual art.

WRITE a scene from a play.

PRESENT your scene to the class.

BIG QUESTION 8

How do we express ourselves?

A **Watch the video. Then talk about it with your partner.**

B **Look at the picture and discuss it with your class.**

1 What kind of picture is this?
2 What are the people doing?

C **Think and answer the questions.**

1 How many ways do people express themselves?
2 What feelings do people express?
3 How do you express yourself?
4 What do people express when they speak or write?

D **Discuss this topic with your class.**
Fill out the Big Question Chart.

UNIT 15 Get Ready

Words

A **Listen and say the words. Then read and listen to the sentences.** 4•02

design | innovative | remarkable | ambitious | permanent | settle | emerge | artificial | promote | enclose | suitable | beneficial

1 The potter **designs** beautiful pottery.
2 **Innovative** ideas are new and fresh.
3 My dad is a **remarkable** man. He's clever and hardworking.
4 I'm **ambitious**. I want to be very successful one day.
5 Something that is **permanent** never goes away.
6 Throughout history, people have **settled** where there's water.
7 New inventions **emerge** every day.
8 That's not natural sugar. It's an **artificial** sweetener.
9 Brushing your teeth every day **promotes** healthy teeth.
10 The animals in the safari park are **enclosed** by high fences.
11 *Treasure Island* is a **suitable** book for children.
12 Eating vegetables is **beneficial** to your health.

B **Match each word to its opposite.**

1 enclosed   2 innovative   3 ambitious   4 artificial   5 harmful   6 temporary

a permanent   b helpful   c open   d old-fashioned   e lazy   f natural

C **Choose the best word to complete each sentence.**

suitable
promotes
emerge
remarkable
settle
design

1 That movie was ______________. I'd never seen anything like it!
2 Some people like the country. Others prefer to ______________ in a city.
3 The calcium in milk ______________ good growth in your bones.
4 The shapes in this painting only ______________ when you look at it for a long time.
5 When I grow up, I want to ______________ clothing.
6 The story was very sweet and ______________ for very young children.

Before You Read

Think Answer the questions.

1 What's a sculpture?

2 Where would you expect to see one?

D **Learn** Taking Notes

As you read, underline the things you think are important in the article. Make some notes on a separate piece of paper. Notes don't have to be whole sentences. You can just write a few words to help you remember what you've read.

Read the passage. Underline four important things. Fill in the chart.

Korky Paul is an artist who illustrates children's books. He was born in Zimbabwe, Africa, and now lives in Oxford, England. He has won several awards for his illustrations, including the Children's Book Award. Korky's illustrations are done in pen, ink, and watercolor paints, and they are known for being very strong and detailed. His work has been compared to Tom and Jerry cartoons, but it's full of jokes and details. Korky's books have sold millions of copies.

Who: ____________________

What: ____________________

When: ____________________

Where: ____________________

E **Words in Context** Scan the text on pages 154–155 and circle these words. As you read, try to guess what the words mean.

cease **magnified** **algae** **applies** **provides** **crustaceans**

F **Look at the pictures on pages 154–155. What do you think is special about this type of art?**

PREVIEW

One Man's Self-Expression

In this *informational text*, you'll read about an artist who makes very special sculptures. An informational text includes facts. You often see this kind of text in schoolbooks, magazines, and on the Internet. As you read, underline the things you think are important and take some notes. This will help you remember the information.

The Arts

Read 4•03

One Man's Self-Expression:

The Mysterious Underwater World of Jason deCaires Taylor

Humans never cease to find innovative ways of expressing themselves. From the early cave paintings that our ancestors drew to the present day, there are millions of examples of self-expression, ranging from music to painting, poetry to dance. They express our feelings as we explore what it means to be human.

Imagine swimming in the sea and suddenly, beneath you, seeing a sculpture of a man sitting at a desk with a typewriter! If you went to Grenada, in the West Indies, that's exactly what you'd see. It's just one of the remarkable ideas that has come out of the mind of Jason deCaires Taylor.

Taylor is a sculptor, but a sculptor with a difference. Instead of putting his sculptures in a park or an art gallery, he puts them underwater and creates "living" sculptures. Taylor chooses areas of the world where there is clear, shallow water. His underwater exhibitions can be seen in Mexico, Grenada, and the United Kingdom. Scuba divers, snorkelers, swimmers, and tourists in glass-bottomed boats can all see this mysterious world that Taylor has created. Underwater, everything is magnified (it looks bigger) and colors change because the only light underwater is from the surface.

One of Taylor's most ambitious exhibitions is *The Silent Evolution*, a permanent artificial reef in Mexico that occupies an underwater space of 420 square meters. It's made up of 400 life-size sculptures of people.

Think
What notes can you make about what you've read so far?

The amazing thing about Taylor's work is that, over time, his sculptures become "living." Algae, a type of ocean plant, begins to grow on the figures, as does coral. Fish swim in between the sculptures; starfish cling to them. The surface of the sculptures changes. At first they look smooth, but later they look bumpy and rough. Different colors emerge as the marine plants settle on their new, man-made habitat. Effectively, the exhibition turns into an artificial coral reef.

Taylor's art is a combination of art and science. He works with marine biologists to create habitats for specific species of marine animals. Each sculpture is made from environmentally friendly materials that promote coral growth and is designed to last for hundreds of years. In an interview, Taylor said, "The coral applies the paint. The fish supply the atmosphere. The water provides the mood. People ask me when it's going to be finished. This is just the beginning."

So, what is Taylor's self-expression? His work looks at humans and nature, loss, and hope. Human activity has destroyed some of the largest, most beautiful coral reefs in the world. In just a few decades, 40 percent of them have disappeared, and scientists predict that 80 percent will have vanished by 2050. By creating artificial reefs, Taylor hopes to draw people away from the natural ones and save them. Taylor also feels that modern technology has meant we have lost things that will never return, like the typewriter, which no one uses anymore because we have computers. His *Lost Correspondent* exhibit expresses this loss.

In his exhibition *The Anthropocene*, which lies on the seabed at a depth of eight meters, Taylor used materials to attract crustaceans such as lobsters, crabs, and shrimp. A life-size copy of a Volkswagen Beetle car encloses a "lobster city." The holes in the bottom part of the car act as doors for the lobsters to swim through, while the holes in the windows are suitable for small fish species to enter the car to hide and to breed. Inside the car, there are living spaces for lobsters. And so, this innovative example of human art turns into something that is positive and beneficial to marine life.

Think
What are the most important things you need to make notes about?

Comprehension

Think Which of Taylor's exhibitions did you find most interesting? Discuss them with your partner.

A Use the chart to make notes about "One Man's Self-Expression." Then compare your notes with your partner's.

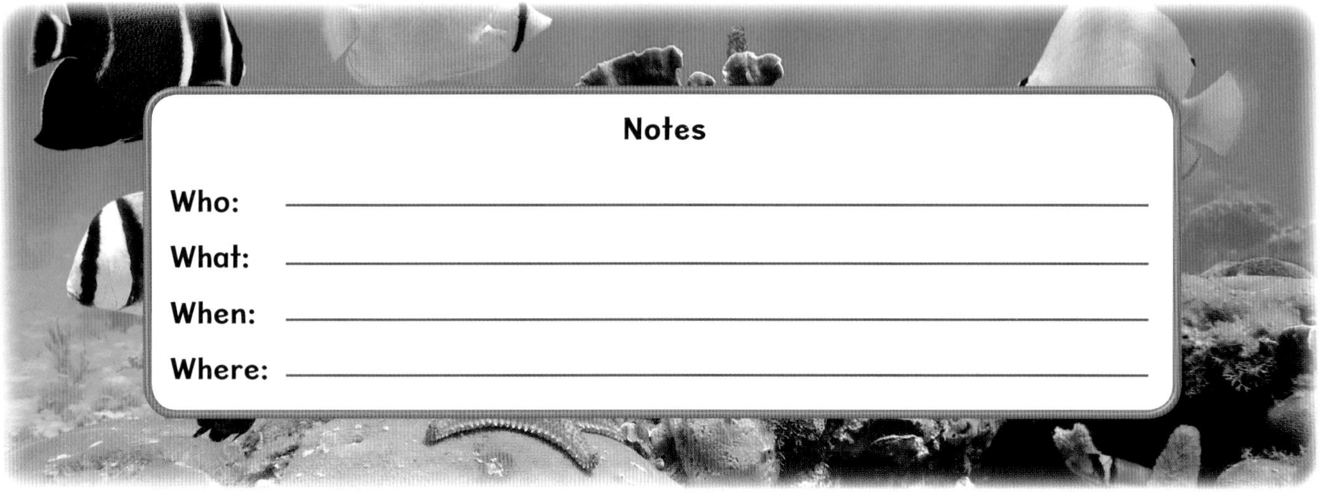

Notes

Who: ______________________

What: ______________________

When: ______________________

Where: ______________________

B Write answers to the questions in your notebook. Then discuss them as a class.

1 What form of art does Jason deCaires Taylor use to express himself?
2 Why does Taylor put his exhibitions underwater?
3 What happens to the sculptures over time?
4 How do the sculptures benefit marine life?
5 Is Taylor's art innovative or old-fashioned?
6 Do you like Taylor's sculptures? Explain why or why not.
7 What do you think Taylor is expressing?

C **Words in Context** Look again at the words you circled in the article. Match each word to its definition.

1 cease	a enlarged
2 magnified	b a type of plant that grows in wet conditions
3 algae	c gives
4 applies	d marine animals, like shrimp and crabs
5 provides	e stop
6 crustaceans	f puts something onto something else

Grammar in Use

D **Listen and read along. Then answer the questions.** 4•04

1 How did Charlie feel?
2 How does the sandwich sound to April?

E **Learn Grammar** Sense Verb + Adjective

Be careful! **Sense verbs** (**look**, **feel**, **sound**, **smell**, **taste**) are followed by an adjective, *not* an adverb.

The sculptures look bumpy and rough.

I felt sick this morning, but I'm OK now.

You look happy!

This lemon smells good, but it tastes bitter.

Your new song sounds fantastic!

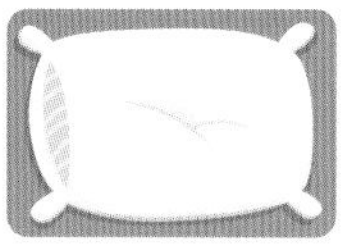

feel / soft

look / angry

taste / delicious

sound / loud

smell / beautiful

Complete each sentence with the correct sense verb.

1 I ______________ tired. I couldn't sleep last night.
2 What's wrong? You ______________ very angry!
3 That machine ______________ like a plane taking off. It's loud!
4 Sue-jin loves roses because they ______________ sweet.
5 Mmm! That ______________ delicious! Is it chocolate?

F **Look at E. Use the pictures and the verb / adjective combinations to make sentences. Practice with your partner.**

Communicate

Listening

Think What things are people proud of?

A **Listen. What instrument does Ramiro play?** 4•05

B **Listen again. Write short answers to the questions.** 4•06

1 When did Ramiro start writing songs? ______________________

2 How old is Ramiro now? ______________________

3 When did Ramiro join The Skaters? ______________________

4 What was Ramiro's proudest moment? ______________________

5 How does Ramiro express himself? ______________________

6 What makes Ramiro happiest? ______________________

Speaking 4•07

C **Work with a partner. What kind of self-expression do you think is the most interesting or important? Ask and answer.**

- art
- music
- poetry
- dance

Word Study

D **Learn** Homophones

Some words sound the same, but they're spelled differently and have different meanings. Here are some of the most common ones.

its / it's   your / you're   their / there   here / hear   who's / whose

The music here is loud. I can't hear you.

Listen, say, and number the words. 4•08 A-Z

____ hear / here   ____ there / their   ____ you're / your

____ whose / who's   ____ its / it's

E **Work with your partner. Write a sentence for each word above.**

Writing Study

F **Learn** Quantifiers

Use most, many, and several to talk about numbers of things when you write. *Most* means almost all, but not all. *Many* means a large number. *Several* means more than two but not a large number.

Most of my friends live in an apartment.
Many of our teachers catch the bus to school.
There are several big buildings in my town.

Complete these sentences about you.

1 Most of my classes ____________________.

2 Many of my friends ____________________.

3 Several people I know ____________________.

Write Now practice writing in the **Workbook.** page 149

BIG QUESTION 8

How do we express ourselves?

UNIT 16 Get Ready

Words

A **Listen and say the words. Then read and listen to the sentences.** 4•09

cabin	advisor	deck	grateful	tempest	save
break up	react	villain	stage	playwright	set

1 The ship has a hundred **cabins** for people to sleep in.
2 Let's ask one of the **advisors** what we should do.
3 Be careful! The ship's **deck** is slippery from the rain.
4 Thank you. I'm very **grateful** for your help.
5 A **tempest** is a very strong storm.
6 The firefighter **saved** the cat stuck in a tree.
7 Sometimes ships are damaged or **broken up** in storms.
8 If you hear something funny, you might **react** by laughing.
9 A **villain** in a play is the one who does bad things.
10 Every theater has a **stage** where the actors perform.
11 The **playwright** wrote a new play every year.
12 The actors performed the play on a beautiful **set**.

B **Circle the one that doesn't belong. Look up any words you don't know in your dictionary.**

1	damage	break up	mend
2	thief	hero	villain
3	advisor	helper	dentist
4	thankful	grateful	angry
5	storm	ocean	tempest
6	playwright	sailor	poet

C **Choose the best word to complete each sentence.**

deck saves stage cabins playwright set reacted

1 The theater had a beautiful ______________ on the ______________.
2 In the play, the captain ______________ his passengers from the storm.
3 A ______________ decides what a play will be about.
4 Some of the play takes place in the ship's ______________, where people sleep.
5 I left my cabin and went to the ship's ______________ for some fresh air.
6 Mom thought the play was funny. She ______________ by laughing.

Before You Read

Think What do you think it's like to be on a ship in a storm?

D **Learn** Making Connections

When you read, think about what you already know about the subject. Think about your own experiences. Have you been in a similar situation? Can you make connections between what you're reading and other texts you've read? Use a chart like the one below to help you.

What do you know about fashion? Fill in the first two columns of the chart. Then read the text and fill in the last column.

Clothes have many different uses. They cover your body and they keep you warm or cool, but they also communicate things about you. Many people express things about themselves through the clothes they choose to wear. For example, if someone likes a particular type of music, they might wear clothes that are similar to the clothes that other followers of that music wear. People who are very confident may wear bright, bold colors, while people who are shy may wear darker or softer colors.

What I Know	What I Want to Know	What I Learned

E **Words in Context** Scan the play on pages 162–163 and circle these words. As you read, try to guess what the words mean.

aid **massive** **petrified** **crew** **elderly** **preventing**

F Look at the picture on pages 162–163. What do you think the play is about?

PREVIEW

The Tempest

This scene is adapted from a play by William Shakespeare (1564–1616), who was a famous English playwright. In this scene, you'll read about a storm at sea. *Drama* is fiction specially written to be performed by actors on a stage. It's usually written in dialogue. As you read, make connections with things you already know. Have you ever been in a storm?

Read 4-10

The Tempest

Drama is a form of self-expression that begins when a playwright writes a play to express feelings about a topic or about life in general. But the play is only the beginning; drama can only happen with the aid of other people. Actors express themselves by performing the play and bringing it to life in their own unique way. Set designers decide how the stage will look during the performance. The audience watching the play also contributes by reacting to the actors and to the lines that are being spoken.

Think
What do you already know about plays? What do you want to know?

One man, who was both a poet and playwright, became the most famous writer in the English language: William Shakespeare. His plays have been performed all over the world, and in many languages.

One of Shakespeare's plays is called *The Tempest*. A tempest is a violent storm. At the beginning of the play, a ship is sailing from Tunis, in North Africa, to Italy. The ship is carrying some extremely important people. When a massive storm starts at sea, everybody on board is petrified that the waves and wind will break up the ship and throw the passengers and crew into the water. The captain and all the sailors are doing their very best to save the ship and its passengers from the storm.

Cast of The Tempest:

Alonso
King of Naples (a city in Italy)

Ferdinand
Alonso's son

Sebastian
Alonso's son and brother of Ferdinand

Antonio
Duke of Milan (another city in Italy)

Gonzalo
an elderly man who is an advisor to the king

Sailors

Act 1, Scene 1

Loud noises of thunder and lightning can be heard because of the terrible storm. A ship's captain and a sailor walk onto the stage.

CAPTAIN: Sailor!

SAILOR: I'm here, captain. How can I help you?

CAPTAIN: Oh, good! Please go and talk to the other sailors. We're in trouble. Talk to the sailors, get them ready. Hurry, before the ship runs into the rocks! Hurry! Go!

The captain leaves the stage, fast. More sailors enter the stage.

SAILOR: Come on, sailors! Good job! Quickly, quickly! You need to take in the big sail. And listen carefully to the captain's orders. Blow until you burst, wind, but leave enough room for us!

Alonso, Sebastian, Antonio, Ferdinand, Gonzalo, and some others enter the stage.

ALONSO: Watch out, good sailor! Where's the captain? Make sure the other sailors do their work.

SAILOR: Please go back under the deck, Sir!

ANTONIO: Sailor, where's the captain?

SAILOR: The captain is busy giving people orders. Can't you hear him? You're preventing us from doing our work. Go back to your cabins. You're helping the storm, not us!

GONZALO: Calm down, good sailor!

SAILOR: It's difficult to calm down in a storm! I'll calm down when the sea calms down! Now go! These big waves don't care about kings and their advisors. Go to your cabin and keep quiet! Don't add to our problems.

GONZALO: I'll do what you say, but just remember, you have important people on board.

SAILOR: The most important person on board is me! If you're so important, then order the storm to stop. If you can calm this weather, and make the sea peaceful, we can put down our ropes and rest. If you cannot, then be grateful for your long life, go to your cabin, and get ready for the worst. Come on, men! Now get out of our way.

The sailor leaves the stage.

GONZALO: That sailor makes me feel better. He'll never die on a ship at sea. We're lucky to be here with a terrible villain like him. If he survives this storm, we all will.

Gonzalo and the other king's advisors leave the stage.

Understand

Comprehension

Think If you could play a part in *The Tempest*, which character would you be? Talk about it with your partner.

A What did you know before you read *The Tempest*? What did you want to know? What have you learned about how we express ourselves? Fill in the chart.

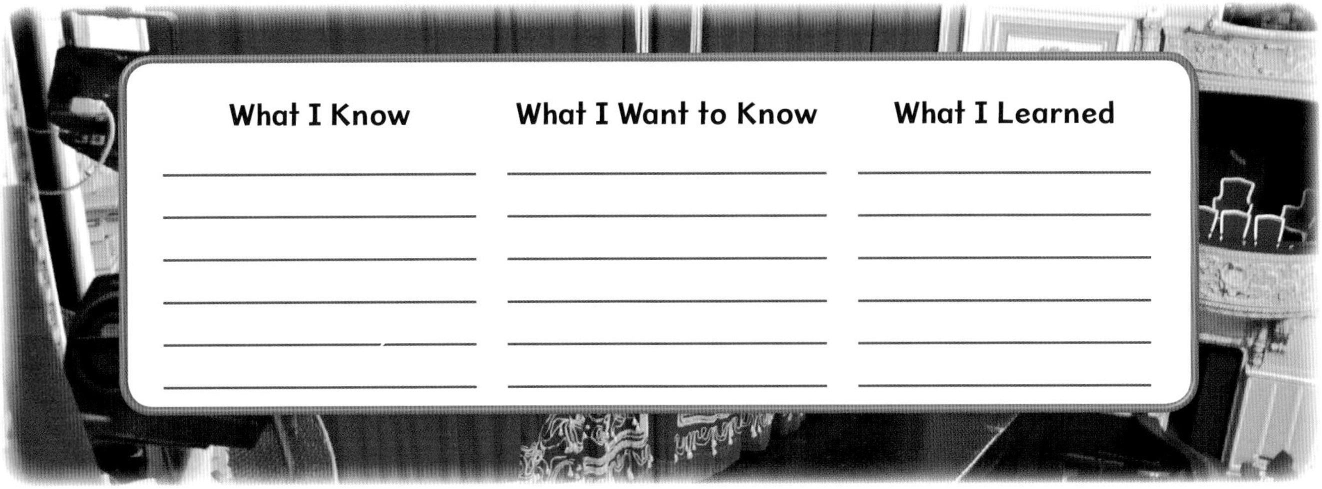

What I Know	What I Want to Know	What I Learned
________________	________________	________________
________________	________________	________________
________________	________________	________________
________________	________________	________________
________________	________________	________________
________________	________________	________________

B Write answers to the questions in your notebook. Then discuss them as a class.

1 Why is the captain worried?
2 What does the captain think might happen to his ship?
3 Who is told to take in the big sail?
4 Where does the sailor tell Alonso and Gonzalo to go?
5 Why does he tell them to go there?
6 Why is the sailor angry with Gonzalo?
7 Why does the sailor make Gonzalo feel better?

C **Words in Context** Look again at the words you circled in the play. Match each definition to its word.

1 another word for *old*	**a** aid
2 very large	**b** massive
3 stopping something or someone	**c** crew
4 another word for *help*	**d** elderly
5 the people who work on a ship	**e** petrified
6 extremely scared	**f** preventing

Grammar in Use

D **Listen and read along. Then circle Yes or No.** 4•11

Charlie thinks it's easy to the climb the tree. Is he right? **Yes** **No**

E **Learn Grammar** **Infinitive as Subject**

Use *it's* + adjective + **infinitive as subject** to express an opinion.

It's difficult to save the passengers and crew.
(Saving the passengers and crew is difficult.)

It's fun to climb a tree.
(Climbing a tree is fun.)

Work with your partner. Take turns telling each other what you think. Use infinitives to express your opinions.

It's difficult ...	It's fun ...	It's easy ...
It's dangerous ...	It's nice ...	It's exciting ...

1 learn to swim
2 speak another language
3 cook a meal
4 ride a horse
5 climb a mountain
6 catch a butterfly
7 solve a mystery
8 do a crossword puzzle

F **Work with your partner. Think of all the things you do at school. Take turns expressing your opinions to each other.**

Communicate

Listening

Think What do you think is good about dancing? Tell the class.

A Listen to a dancer talk about dancing. Check (✓) the statements you hear. 4•12

- ☐ I've been dancing since I was six.
- ☐ I dance to keep fit.
- ☐ I enjoy dressing up in beautiful costumes.
- ☐ I feel I'm giving a gift to the audience.
- ☐ I smile when I dance.
- ☐ It's natural for people to move rhythmically.
- ☐ Everybody dances slowly.
- ☐ When you're happy, you might dance faster.

B Listen again. Write a sentence that explains what it means to dance rhythmically. 4•13

Speaking 4•14

C **Learn** Expressing Thanks

Express thanks by using these expressions:

- Thank you so much.
- I appreciate it.
- That's very kind of you.

Talk about one of these topics with your partner. Take turns being kind and offering thanks.

- **sharing candy**
- **returning a lost phone**
- **helping with math**

Word Study

D **Learn** Verb + Preposition

Some verbs are always followed by a preposition such as **for**, **to**, or **about**.

I'm going to study for my test.

Do you want to talk about the plan?

Listen, say, and number the words. Then use the verbs and their prepositions in sentences. 4•15 A-Z

____ work for	____ belong to	____ talk about	____ apologize for
____ think about	____ study for	____ care for	____ ask for

Writing Study

E **Learn** Semicolons

Use **semicolons** to connect two independent clauses that are related in meaning. This means you can join sentences without adding words like **and**, **but**, or **yet**.

I saw an artist on TV. She won a prize.

I saw an artist on TV; she won a prize.

I saw an artist on TV, and she won a prize.

Rewrite the sentences using semicolons.

1 Jamie threw the ball. It hit a window.

____

2 I didn't want help, and I didn't ask for it.

____

3 The teacher liked my homework. She suggested two changes.

____

____

Write Now practice writing in the **Workbook**. page 157

Wrap Up

Writing

A **Read this scene from a play.**

Scene and setting — *[Sailors 1, 2, 3, and 4 are standing on deck, looking out to sea. The captain is steering the ship and looking at his / her map.]*

Stage direction — Sailor 1: *[Stretches out his / her arms and looks very happy.]*

Character lines —

Sailor 1: What a beautiful day! The sun is hot, and there's a good wind for our sails. I wonder where our ship will take us today.

Sailor 2: I'm sure the captain knows. Let's ask him.

Sailor 1: Captain, where are we heading today?

Captain: *[Smiles.]* You'll find out in an hour or so. You're going to love it!

Sailor 3: Cool! Maybe we'll find a harbor in a big city.

Sailor 4: Yes! Or maybe we'll see mountains and rivers.

Sailor 2: *[Looks very excited and jumps up and down.]*
Or maybe, just maybe, we'll land on a desert island ...

Sailor 1: Oh, yes! With palm trees and coconuts!

Sailor 3: And a sandy beach and clear blue water to swim in!

Sailor 2: Hey! Watch out for that big wave! Get your ropes!

Captain: All crew on deck, please!

[All sailors run to the deck and pick up their ropes.]

Captain: Pull in the main sail. We're turning.

[All sailors pull hard on the ropes to turn the ship away from the waves and into the wind.]

Sailor 1: Look! Look! An island. It's fantastic. It's like a dream!

B **Answer the questions.**

1 Where does the playwright set the scene?
2 How do the actors know what to do?
3 Who speaks in the scene?

C Learn Writing a Scene from a Play

- Choose a setting for your play. This could be anywhere you feel like writing about: a beach, a shopping mall, a school, a park, on a plane, or on a boat.
- Give directions for the director and actors. Write them in the present tense.
- Include lines for several actors. The actors' lines keep the story moving. To keep the play exciting, several actors can say things, not just one or two.

Write Now go to the **Workbook** to plan and write the first scene of a play. page 159

D Practice performing your scene. Then perform your scene for the class.

1 Form small groups. Practice reading your lines aloud.
2 Decide if you need any props (objects).
3 Before you begin, have one cast member tell the class where your scene takes place.
4 Start the scene. Remember to pay attention to stage directions.
5 When it's time to say your lines, say them in a loud, clear voice.
6 Use gestures, and exit and enter on time.
7 Enjoy yourself! If you have fun, the audience will, too!

BIG QUESTION 8

How do we express ourselves?

A Watch the video. How do you see people expressing themselves?

B What are some answers to the Big Question? Talk about them with your partner.

C Complete the **Big Question Chart**. Then discuss it with the class.

In units **17** and **18** you will:

WATCH a video about buildings.

LEARN about different kinds of buildings.

READ about beautiful and unusual buildings.

WRITE a magazine article.

PRESENT your article to the class.

BIG QUESTION 9

Why do we make buildings?

A **Watch the video. Then talk about it with your partner.**

B **Look at the picture and discuss it with your class.**

1 What kinds of buildings are these?
2 Why are there so many different kinds of buildings?

C **Think and answer the questions.**

1 What kind of building do you live in?
2 Why do we need buildings?
3 How many kinds of buildings can you name?
4 What's your favorite kind of building?

D **Discuss this topic with your class. Fill out the Big Question Chart.**

UNIT 17 Get Ready

Words

A Listen and say the words. Then read and listen to the sentences. 4•16

stadium	lighthouse	tower	skyscraper	warehouse	palace
courthouse	theater	concert hall	office	art gallery	showroom

1 You can play many kinds of sports in a **stadium**.
2 The old **lighthouse** kept ships away from the rocks.
3 You could see the tall **towers** from a long way away.
4 New York City is famous for its huge **skyscrapers**.
5 New books are stored in the **warehouse**.
6 In the past, kings and queens lived in **palaces**. Some still do!
7 Judges and lawyers go to the **courthouse** every day.
8 She went to the **theater** to see a new play.
9 The musicians will perform in the **concert hall** tonight.
10 Many business people work in an **office**.
11 He's showing his paintings at an **art gallery** next week.
12 The new car was displayed in a **showroom**.

B Complete the chart. Some words can go in more than one column.

stadium lighthouse tower skyscraper warehouse palace
courthouse theater concert hall office art gallery showroom

Buildings for Sleeping	Buildings for Working	Buildings for Entertainment

C Talk with your partner. Answer the questions.

1 What buildings do you go to for fun?
2 What buildings do you go to when you want to learn something?
3 What buildings do you think are most useful?

Before You Read

Think Who designs buildings?

D **Learn** Sequence of Events

When you read, think about the order in which things happen.

- What happens first? What happens next?
- Why does one event happen before another?
- What's the result of these events?

Use a chart like the one below to help you sequence the events.

Read the paragraph. Think about the sequence of events. Then fill in the chart.

To build a tree house, you need to choose a strong and healthy tree. Then, list what materials you will use to build the tree house. Now you can draw a plan to show what your house will look like. Will it have a roof and windows? When the plan is finished, you can buy the materials and then build, starting with the floor. Next, add the walls and roof. Now it's time to add a ladder so you can get into the house. Finally, it's time to move in!

1 ____________________

2 ____________________

3 ____________________

4 ____________________

5 ____________________

6 ____________________

7 ____________________

8 ____________________

E **Words in Context** Scan the article on pages 174–175 and circle these words. As you read, try to guess what the words mean.

function **steel** **architect** **countless** **construction** **aquatics**

F Look at the pictures on pages 174–175. Which building would you most like to live or work in?

PREVIEW

The World's Most Extraordinary Buildings

In this *magazine article*, you'll read about interesting buildings around the world. Magazine articles usually give you information about a subject. They often include illustrations, photos, and diagrams. As you read, think about the sequence of events. This will help you understand how people make buildings.

Social Studies: Technology

Read 4•17

The World's Most Extraordinary Buildings

So, a building is just a building, right? Wrong! Buildings have many different purposes. People use buildings for living, for working, for manufacturing, and also for going to school or to the movies. Here are some of the key reasons we build buildings.

Buildings for Shelter

Everybody needs a place to sleep, eat, and keep themselves protected from the weather, so we build houses, apartments, and hotels. Have a look at a few exceptional ones from around the world.

The Palais Bulles (Bubble Palace) is a "palace" that's used for conferences and other big events. It reminds people of caves; there aren't any straight lines at all.

This house in Mexico was built to look and feel like the inside of a snail's shell.

There's a hotel in Finland that's made entirely of glass igloos where guests can sleep under the stars.

And take a look at this hotel in the Maldives. Its bedrooms are almost 5 meters underwater!

Buildings for Work

People have jobs, so they need places where they can work. People work in factories, warehouses, lighthouses, offices, schools, hospitals, courthouses, restaurants, airports, barns, showrooms, libraries, skyscrapers, and bus, train, fire, and police stations.

This is the headquarters of the Longaberger Company in Ohio, which manufactures wooden baskets.

Here's an office with a difference! It recycles water and uses the power of the sun. There are even trees growing on a terrace on one of the floors.

Buildings for Leisure and Fun

Everyone likes to have fun, so we need buildings for that purpose, too, whether we want to listen to a concert, go to a play, or play some sports. Shopping malls, movie theaters, and museums are all buildings that we use for having fun.

This incredible museum is built in the shape of a saucer. It's set on a clifftop above a beach in Niterói, Brazil.

What Do Architects Do?

Before a building can be built, an architect needs to design the shape of the building and plan exactly how it will be used. First, the architect has to consider how many people will need to work or live inside the building and what activities these people will be doing. This is called the function of the building. Then the architect draws detailed plans and makes a model of the building so that clients can see what the finished structure will look like. This also helps the architect decide how much steel will be needed. When the planning is finished and approved, construction can begin.

Think
What is the sequence of events?

Meet the Architect

Zaha Hadid is an architect who has designed countless buildings: concert halls, theaters, towers, museums, art galleries, stadiums, ski jumps with cafés ... you name it! Here are some of Zaha's most famous buildings:

The Dorobanti Tower, in the heart of Bucharest, Hungary, is an apartment block that was designed using diamond shapes and stands 200 meters tall. It's visible from several kilometers away and has been designed to be extremely strong, since Bucharest is located in an earthquake zone.

In 2002, construction of the Bergisel ski jump in Innsbruck, Austria, was completed. Zaha's vision was to extend the natural mountain slope into the sky above. The jump contains sports facilities, a café, and a viewing terrace. Zaha was also the architect for the London Olympics Aquatics Centre, where all the swimming and diving competitions took place.

Check this out! It's part of the Dongdaemun Design Plaza and Park, designed by Zaha to bring inspiration to the people of Seoul, South Korea. It has a design museum, a library, and lecture theaters. It's surrounded by a 30,000-square-meter park laid out in the traditional Korean way with reflecting pools, lotus ponds, and bamboo plants.

Understand

Comprehension

Think Which building in the magazine article was your favorite? Which was your least favorite? Talk about them with your partner.

A Look at the sequence of events in the "What Do Architects Do?" section of the article. Then fill in the chart.

1 ______________________

2 ______________________

3 ______________________

4 ______________________

5 ______________________

6 ______________________

B Answer the questions. Then discuss them as a class.

1 What is an architect's job?
2 What things does an architect need to think about before designing a building?
3 How many key reasons are given for building buildings? What are the reasons?
4 What do you think of Zaha Hadid's designs?
5 What kind of building would you like to build? What would it look like?

C **Words in Context** Look again at the words you circled in the article. Then write them in the correct sentences.

1 Protecting people from the weather is an important ______________ of a building.
2 ______________ is used to make many things, including doors and window frames.
3 There are ______________ ways to design buildings.
4 Most buildings are designed by an ______________.
5 ______________ are sports that take place in or on water.
6 Before ______________ begins, engineers study the architect's plan.

Workbook Grammar
pages 166–167

Grammar in Use

D Listen and read along. Then circle the correct answer. 4•18

Why does Charlie say "the" pool?

a There are many pools. **b** There is only one pool.

E Learn Grammar ***A, An, The,*** **and No Article**

Use **a** or **an** the first time you talk about something. Use **the** when you talk about it again.

Before a building can be built, the building needs to be designed.

Use **a** or **an** with things that aren't special.

It's a kangaroo. (This one isn't special.)

Use **the** when the person you're talking to knows what you're talking about.

It's in the pool. (The person knows which pool.)

Don't use an article to talk about sports, meals, most countries, and school subjects.

I play tennis. I saw Jim at lunch. We went to Spain. They like math.

Correct the sentences. Add *a, an,* or *the* if you need to.

1 Do you like swimming? Yes, I do. I go to ***the*** pool every weekend.
2 Can I have apple, please? Sure, there's apple in fridge.
3 What's that? It's elephant.
4 What are you eating for lunch? I'll have sandwich. Sandwiches my mom makes are great.

F Look at E. Ask and answer the questions with your partner.

Communicate

Listening

Think Do you know what lighthouses are used for? Why are they important?

A **Listen and circle the correct answers.** 4•19

1 Bob was a lighthouse keeper for **thirty-two years / two years / thirty years.**

2 One function of a lighthouse is to warn sailors of **whales / bad weather / dangerous rocks.**

3 A lighthouse also helps ships find their way home **in the daytime / at night / in good weather.**

4 Lighthouses show ships the way back to **their towns / the hotel / the harbor.**

B **Listen again and discuss as a class. Do lighthouses use lighthouse keepers now? What are lighthouses used for today?** 4•20

Speaking 4•21

C **Take turns asking questions and talking about the place where you'd like to live. Support your reasons with phrases like *I believe, I think,* or *What I like about*.**

- lighthouse
- apartment
- palace
- house
- skyscraper

Word Study

D **Learn** More Phrasal Verbs

Some verbs are used with words such as across, way, down, for, in, off, out, up, and with. These two-part verbs are called phrasal verbs. The word that comes after the verb changes the meaning.

Phrasal Verb	Meaning	Example
go on	continue	**The lesson went on for an hour.**
go back	return	**I want to go back home now.**
go up	increase	**The price of movie tickets went up last month.**

Listen, say, and number the phrasal verbs. Then write a sentence using each one. 4•22 A-Z

____ go on ____ go back ____ go up ____ lie down

____ put down ____ catch up ____ pick up ____ fall off

Writing Study

E **Learn** Run-On Sentences

A run-on sentence is two complete sentences that run together.
I don't like tall buildings they scare me.

You can fix a run-on sentence by separating the clauses with a semicolon or a period or by adding a conjunction.

I don't like tall buildings; they scare me.
I don't like tall buildings because they scare me.

Write S (sentence) or R (run-on sentence).

1 The enormous glass and steel skyscraper moves slightly when the wind is very stong. ________
2 Lighthouses are extremely important they protect sailors and their ships. ________
3 It's going to be a hot day put on some sunscreen so you won't get a sunburn. ________

Write Now practice writing in the **Workbook**. page 169

BIG QUESTION 9

Why do we make buildings?

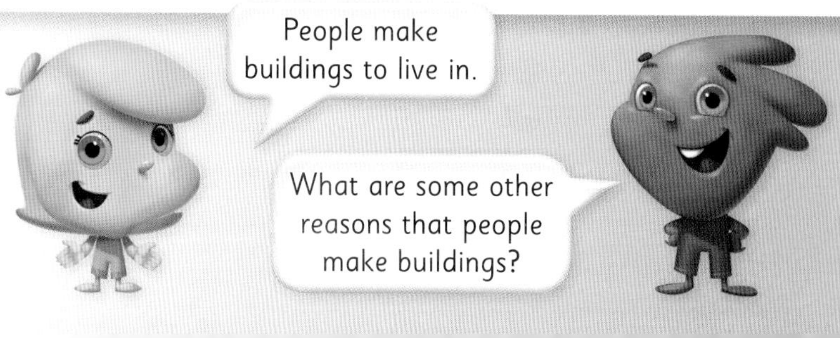

UNIT 18 Get Ready

Words

A Listen and say the words. Then read and listen to the sentences. 4•23

turrets | stables | gatehouse | moat | drawbridge | hall

courtyard | ramparts | mumble | stiffen | missing | tremble

1 Do you see those tall **turrets**? They look like towers.
2 The horses live in the **stables**.
3 To get into a castle, people have to pass by the **gatehouse**.
4 The **moat** was deep and filled with water.
5 The **drawbridge** was lowered so that the king could enter the castle.
6 The king and queen ate in the castle **hall**.
7 A chilly wind blew through the big, empty **courtyard**.
8 The castle had **ramparts** high up around its edge.
9 It's difficult to hear someone who **mumbles**.
10 My back **stiffened** because I'd been sitting down too long.
11 I may have lost my jacket. It's **missing**.
12 Why did you **tremble**? Were you scared?

B Look at the picture and number the words.

____ turrets
____ stables
____ gatehouse
____ moat
____ drawbridge
____ hall
____ courtyard
____ ramparts

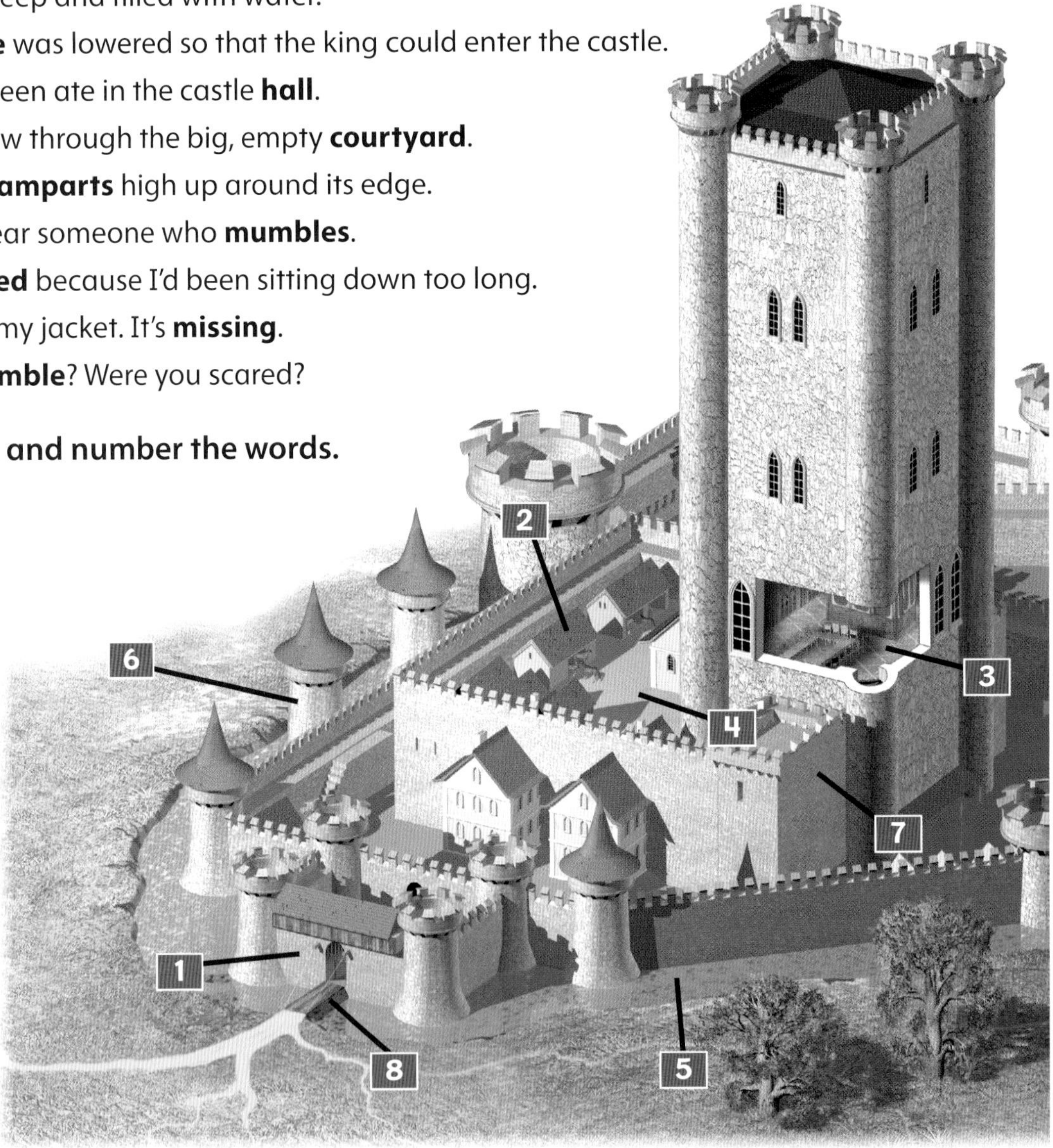

C Write sentences using each of these words: *stiffen*, *mumble*, and *tremble*.

Before You Read

Think Have you ever read a mystery story? What was it about?

D **Learn** Making Predictions

When you read a story, think about what will happen next. What clues are there in the story? What do you already know? Make a prediction about what will happen and then see if your prediction is right.

Use a chart like the one below to help you make predictions.

Read the story and make a prediction. How will the story end? Fill in the predictions chart.

There was the smallest bump and then a horrible noise. Was it metal ripping away from the ship? Or was it an animal groaning in pain? The crew of the ship had never heard such a noise. The captain hadn't, either. Whatever it was, it was extremely unusual. He glanced at the control panel. Everything seemed to be normal. Suddenly, there was laughter coming from the passenger deck below. Passengers had gathered to play with huge pieces of ice. "Where did those come from? Oh no, it can't be!" the captain thought.

Story Clues	→	What I Know	→	My Prediction
______		______		______
______		______		______
______		______		______
______		______		______
______		______		______
______		______		______

E **Words in Context** Scan the story on pages 182–183 and circle these words. As you read, try to guess what the words mean.

solve **surrounded** **gazed** **padlock** **mysterious** **vanished**

F Turn to pages 182–183. Look at the pictures. What do you think the story is about? Make a predictions chart and fill it in as you read the story.

PREVIEW

The Mystery of Peril Castle

In this *mystery* story, a boy has a problem to solve. A mystery is a story about something that happened that is difficult to explain. It has characters, a setting, a plot, and clues. The answer to the mystery is what the characters and readers have to discover. As you read, try to predict what will happen next.

The Mystery of Peril Castle

Peril Castle was built in the 15th century to defend Hellenbore City, but now it was deserted. It had been empty for over a hundred years. The local people didn't dare go near it. Its turrets looked terrifying against the evening sky.

"Thomas!" shouted Thomas's uncle Robert from the attic where he'd been looking through old boxes.

"What is it?" asked Thomas.

"Look! It's proof that Peril Castle belongs to us!" replied Uncle Robert. "Here's the first half of our name!" In his trembling hand was half a gold coin with the letters D-A-W clearly visible on it. Thomas and Robert's last name was Dawson. Also on the coin was half of an eagle's body with its left wing spread wide. Thomas had known all his life that Peril Castle was his family's castle, but without proof, Uncle Robert couldn't claim it.

"We need the other half of the coin. Let's see if we can find it," said Uncle Robert urgently. They ran out of the house and up the hill toward Peril Castle.

Think
What's Thomas going to do? How do you know?

Thomas felt nervous, but they had to solve the mystery of the missing half coin. His knees were trembling as he walked toward the deep moat that surrounded the castle. It was filled with green algae. Robert pulled a lever and the drawbridge swung down, making Thomas jump.

They scurried across the drawbridge. Thomas and Uncle Robert searched the gatehouse and the stables but they found nothing. Then they went into the hall. Hurriedly, they checked every corner, searching for clues that would bring them closer to their goal.

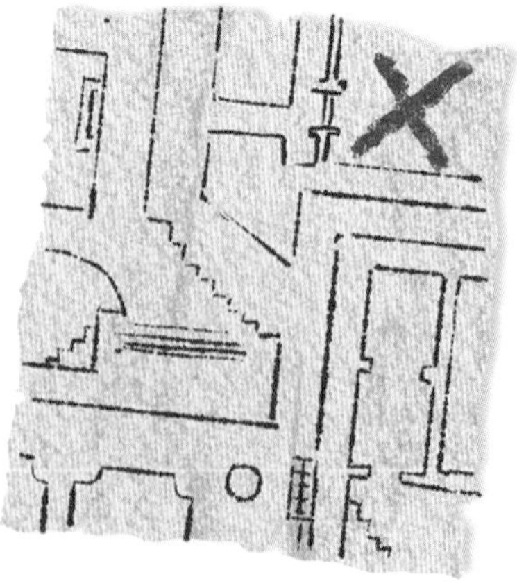

Where shall we look now? thought Thomas, staring at the courtyard. He gazed at the gray stones of the walls and looked up at the ramparts. Then he spotted an ancient metal ladder.

Thomas climbed quickly, listening to his heart thumping. Pulling himself onto the ramparts, he saw a box with a rusty padlock on it.

"I've found a box!" shouted Thomas, shaking the lock. As his uncle scrambled up the ladder, the lid sprang open. At first the box looked empty,

but on closer examination, Thomas saw a secret drawer. He slid it open and found an old map of the castle.

Uncle Robert and Thomas studied the map, which showed the castle as it had originally been built.

"Look!" yelled Thomas. "There's a secret passageway behind the ramparts. It goes right inside the eleventh turret."

As they walked round the ramparts, Thomas noticed a magpie flying back and forth from the eleventh turret. His heart started to thump again, and his body stiffened with anticipation.

Halfway along the ramparts, the pair saw a mysterious crack in the wall. Uncle Robert reached into his bag and took out a hammer. He hit the crack several times, and suddenly a narrow door swung open. As Thomas was watching Uncle Robert, the magpie returned and vanished through a small hole above their heads.

"It's the passageway!" whispered Thomas, squeezing through the narrow door.

"What do you see?" asked Uncle Robert anxiously.

"Nothing. It's too dark!" replied Thomas.

He fumbled around for several minutes until he felt something. It was a pile of objects of different shapes and sizes. Thomas filled his pockets and crawled back out.

Think

What's going to happen next? Why do you think that?

"Look at these shiny things the magpie has collected!" he shouted. There was a key, a Roman coin, a piece of silver, a ring, a spoon, and a tiny mirror.

"What's this?" said Thomas brushing dirt off a lump of metal. "Wait! I don't believe it!"

Thomas turned the metal over, and there, clear as day, were the letters S-O-N and an eagle's right wing. Uncle Robert passed Thomas the other half of the coin that he'd found in the attic. The two halves clicked together as if they'd never been parted. DAWSON! This was the proof they needed!

For a year, Uncle Robert and Thomas proudly restored the fortress. Once the job was done, they renamed it Peril-Dawson Castle. Flying the family flag from the eleventh turret, they invited all the local people to celebrate Hellenbore's ancient castle with them.

Comprehension

Think What two things did you enjoy about "The Mystery of Peril Castle"? Talk with your partner.

A **Look at the prediction chart you completed as you read. Copy its contents here. Then discuss your predictions with the class.**

Story Clues	→	What I Know	→	My Prediction
______		______		______
______		______		______
______		______		______
______		______		______
______		______		______
______		______		______

B **Read each set of three sentences. Circle the sentences that are true.**

1 **a** Thomas wanted to solve a mystery about an eagle.
  b Thomas wanted to know why Peril Castle was empty.
  c Thomas wanted to find the other half of a coin.

2 **a** Thomas climbed onto the castle ramparts.
  b Thomas didn't go into the gatehouse.
  c Thomas jumped into the moat.

3 **a** The magpie collected the other half of the coin.
  b The magpie flew into the hall.
  c The magpie opened the box.

C **Words in Context** **Look again at the words you circled in the story. Then write them in the correct sentences.**

1 One moment it was there, and then it ______________.
2 Tall trees ______________ the old house.
3 We ______________ at the beautiful sunset.
4 We couldn't figure out where the map was hidden. It was ______________!
5 Can you ______________ this puzzle? I can't!
6 I put a ______________ on the gate so no one could open it.

Workbook Grammar pages 174–175

Grammar in Use

D **Listen and read along. Then check (✓) the correct answer.** 4•25

What are Sonya and April going to do now? play video games ☐ play soccer ☐

E **Learn Grammar** Review of Tenses and Future Forms

Remember: Use different tenses and future forms to describe different times.

Past	**I needed to find the coin.** **They had to solve the mystery.**
Present	**I like castles with turrets.** **We need the other half of the coin.**
Future	**Are you going to explore Peril Castle?** **I will see the castles of Wales someday.**

Read the situations. Circle the best answer for each one.

1 You're telling someone what you do every day. What do you say?
 a I was eating breakfast every day. b I eat breakfast every day.

2 You see big black clouds in the sky. What do you say?
 a It will rain. b It's going to rain.

3 You're telling a friend what you did yesterday. What do you say?
 a I went to the mall. b I had gone to the mall.

F **Talk with your partner. Take turns asking and answering questions about *yesterday*, *today*, and *tomorrow*.**

Communicate

Listening

Think Do people all over the world live in the same kinds of houses?

A Listen. What kind of house is the man describing? 4•26

B Listen again. Circle True (T) or False (F). 4•27

1 People who live in traditional Japanese houses don't sleep in beds. T F

2 People in traditional Japanese houses sleep on futons. T F

3 People always remove their shoes before coming into the house. T F

4 Often people wear "house shoes" or slippers. T F

5 Tatami mats are made of plastic and metal. T F

6 A tatami mat is cool in the summer and warm in the winter. T F

Speaking 4•28

C **Learn** Accepting or Refusing Invitations

To accept invitations, say:

- Thanks! That sounds fun.
- Sure. Thank you for the invitation.
- Yes, I'd love to!

To refuse invitations, say:

- No, thank you.
- Thanks, but I'm busy that day.
- I can't. I'm sorry.

Work with your partner. Take turns inviting and accepting or refusing an invitation to one of these events.

- **a party**
- **a tennis game**
- **a boat ride**

Word Study

D **Learn** Adjectives Ending in *-ing*

Make adjectives from verbs by adding -ing.

bore → **boring**
terrify → **terrifying**

That movie is terrifying. It will terrify you.

Listen and say the words. Write the words by adding *-ing*. If a verb ends in an *e* cross out the last letter. 4•29 A-Z

1 dare ____________________
2 please ____________________
3 fascinate ____________________
4 charm ____________________
5 embarrass ____________________
6 surprise ____________________
7 confuse ____________________
8 frighten ____________________

E **Work with your partner to write a paragraph using at least four of the adjectives. Read your paragraph to the class.**

Writing Study

F **Learn** Order of Adjectives

If you use more than one adjective in a sentence, you need to put the adjectives in a special order.

Opinion	Size	Age	Shape	Color	Origin	Material	Purpose	Noun
beautiful		old			Chinese			vase
	huge		round			metal		bowl
	small			yellow			paint	

Put the adjectives in the correct order.

1 big horrible black cloud
____

2 Indian old beautiful building
____

3 brown round leather basketball
____

4 golden scary enormous eagle
____

Write Now practice writing in the **Workbook**. page 177

Wrap Up

Writing

A Read this magazine article.

The Mirrorcube

Hook — Check out this cool building! It's a tree house!

Details — Have you ever wished you could live in the forest, admiring nature by day and night? Well, now you can! This remarkable tree house is available for anyone to buy or rent. Designed by Scandinavian architects, the Mirrorcube is an amazing sight to see ... but you can't see it! It's a box of glass that reflects back everything around it: the trees, the grass, and paths through the forest. "Doesn't that make it dangerous for birds? Won't they fly into it?" you might ask. No! These guys have thought of everything. A clever sheet of film that's invisible to us but visible to birds and animals is hidden inside the glass.

The Mirrorcube looks as if it's hanging in the air. But in fact, it's built around living trees and held on the ground by strong wires. A wooden ladder leads up to the door.

How would you like to spend a night here? It's an environmentally friendly dream!

Mirrorcube facts — Facts

Name:
The Mirrorcube

Architects:
Tham and Videgård

Materials:
Glass, aluminum, and wood

Number of windows:
Six

Number of beds:
One

B Answer the questions.

1 What does the article begin with?
2 How is the box of facts useful?
3 What kinds of details does the article include?

C **Learn** Writing a Magazine Article

- Start your article with a hook. A hook is an interesting sentence that will quickly get the reader interested in your article.
- Choose a topic that is interesting to you. If you're interested in your topic, it'll be fun!
- Research your topic and make a list of things you find interesting. What would the reader most enjoy reading about?
- Gather a short list of facts and display them in your article in a separate section. This could be a caption to a picture or just a box of facts.

Write Now go to the **Workbook** to plan and write your own magazine article. page 179

D Plan your presentation. Then share your magazine article with the class.

1 Once you've written your article, think of what you can do to illustrate it. Add captions or labels for your illustrations.
2 Show your illustrated article to the class before you read. Explain why you chose your topic.
3 Read your article.
4 After you've read it, ask the class what they found interesting.
5 Do your best to answer any questions your classmates have.

BIG QUESTION 9

Why do we make buildings?

A Watch the video. What kinds of buildings do you see?

B What are some answers to the Big Question? Talk about them with your partner.

C Complete the **Big Question Chart**. Then discuss it with the class.

Testing Practice 3

Reading and Writing

A **Read the article. Are sentences 1-4 right (a) or wrong (b)? If there is not enough information to answer *right* (a) or *wrong* (b), choose *doesn't say* (c). Circle your answer.**

Hello! My name is Minoru. I was born in Japan, but I have lived in Germany since I was two years old. I've seen remarkable changes here during my life. In 1955, we only had a theater, a bakery, and a clothing store. Now we have so much. We have a department store, electric buses, a small university, and many new apartment buildings. We even have a skyscraper! Our money has changed, too. We used to use the Deutsche Mark. Now we use the Euro.

1 Minoru was born in Denmark.
a right **b** wrong **c** doesn't say

2 Minoru's town used to have a restaurant.
a right **b** wrong **c** doesn't say

3 There aren't any tall buildings in Minoru's town.
a right **b** wrong **c** doesn't say

4 Minoru uses the Euro as money.
a right **b** wrong **c** doesn't say

B **Read the invitation from your friend Sam.**

It's my birthday! Please come to a party at my house on Sunday, July 30th, at 4:00 p.m. We will have snacks and ice cream. There will be fun games, too.

Please write back by July 25.

Sam

Tip
Use adverbs of degree in your response, such as *very, really, extremely,* and *absolutely*.

Write a note in your notebook and thank Sam for the invitation. Tell him if you will go to the party or not. Write 25–30 words.

Listening

C **You will hear a girl talking about a party. You will hear the recording twice. Then fill in the blanks below.** 4•30

1 Katy was ____________________.
2 Sarah spoke ____________________ and ____________________.
3 Emma spoke ____________________. She was ____________________.
4 Julia spoke ____________________ at first.
5 The conversation was ____________________.

D **Listen to a conversation. You will hear the conversation twice. There are two questions. Put a check (✓) by each right answer.** 4•31

1 What is Luke's English class going to do?

a 
b 
c 

2 Where is there a small stage?

a 
b 
c 

Speaking

Part 1 **Work with a partner. Ask and answer questions about activities in your free time.**

1 What is your favorite sporting activity?
2 What kinds of music do you enjoy?
3 Would you rather read a book or go for a bike ride? Why is that your choice?
4 What do you think you'll be doing in 10 years?

Tip
When it's your turn to answer the questions, use adjectives to describe your home.

Part 2 **Your teacher will give you a sheet of paper with some information on it. One of you will get questions and one of you will get answers. Ask and answer with your partner.**

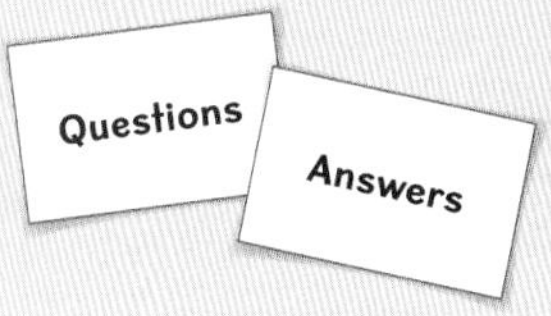

Definitions based on the *Oxford American Dictionary for Learners of English*.

A

accurate ***adj.*** careful and exact; without mistakes

achievement ***noun*** something that is done successfully, especially through hard work or skill

active ***adj.*** able and willing to do things; full of energy

adjustable ***adj.*** that can be moved to different positions or changed in shape or size

adjusted ***verb*** changed something slightly, especially because it was not in the right position

adorable ***adj.*** very attractive and easy to love

advanced ***adj.*** highly developed

adventurous ***adj.*** liking to try new things or have adventures

advisor ***noun*** a person who gives advice to a student, company, government, etc.

aggressively ***adv.*** in a way that shows you are ready to fight or argue

agreement ***noun*** a contract or decision that two or more people have made together

aid ***verb*** to help someone

alarm ***verb*** to make someone or something feel suddenly afraid or worried

algae ***noun*** very simple plants that grow mainly in water

altitude ***noun*** the height of something above sea level

ambitious ***adj.*** having a strong desire to be successful, to have power, etc.

ancient ***adj.*** [1] belonging to or connected with the distant past [2] having existed for a long time

antibiotic ***noun*** a medicine that is used for destroying bacteria and curing infections

apologize for ***verb*** to say that you are sorry for something that you have done

applies ***verb*** puts or spreads something onto a surface

approach ***verb*** to come near or nearer to someone or something

aquatics ***noun*** sports that take place in water

arch ***noun*** a structure made with two columns joined over the top in a curve

architect ***noun*** a person whose job is to design buildings

art gallery ***noun*** a room or building for showing works of art, especially to the public

artificial ***adj.*** not genuine or natural but made by people

ask for ***verb*** to say that you want someone to give you something

assessment ***noun*** the act of judging or forming an opinion about someone or something

atmosphere ***noun*** the mixture of gases that surrounds the Earth or any other star, planet, etc.

attract ***verb*** to cause someone to like or be interested in someone or something

attractive ***adj.*** pleasant to look at; that pleases or interests you; that you like

avoidable ***adj.*** that can be prevented; unnecessary

awestruck ***adj.*** feeling very impressed by something

axle ***noun*** a bar that connects a pair of wheels on a vehicle

B

bank ***noun*** an organization that keeps money safely for its customers; the office or building of such an organization

barter ***verb*** to exchange goods or services for other goods or services, not for money

beamed ***verb*** smiled happily

behave ***verb*** to act in a particular way

belong to ***phrasal verb*** to be owned by someone

beneficial ***adj.*** improving a situation; having a good or useful effect

benefit ***verb*** to have a good or useful effect

bill ***noun*** a piece of paper money

biologist ***noun*** a scientist who studies biology

blurry ***adj.*** not clear

booming ***adj.*** (of a sound or voice) loud, deep, and hollow

borrow ***verb*** to take or receive something from someone or something that you intend to give back, usually after a short time

bravely ***adv.*** in a way that shows you are not afraid

break down ***phrasal verb*** (used about a vehicle or machine) to stop working

break into ***phrasal verb*** to enter a building by force, usually in order to steal something

break off ***phrasal verb*** to suddenly stop doing or saying something

break up ***phrasal verb*** to separate into parts

bright ***adj.*** intelligent; able to learn things quickly

C

cabin ***noun*** a small wooden house in the country

calmly ***adv.*** in a calm way

canine ***noun*** one of the four pointed teeth in the front of a person's or animal's mouth

care for ***phrasal verb*** [1] to help someone who is sick or old and do things for him/her [2] to like or love someone or something

carnivore ***noun*** any animal that eats meat

carnivorous ***adj.*** (of an animal) meat-eating

catch up ***phrasal verb*** to reach someone or something who is ahead of you

cautious ***adj.*** taking great care to avoid possible danger

cavity ***noun*** a hole in a tooth

cease ***verb*** to stop or end

centigrade ***adj.*** another word for Celsius. The name of a scale for measuring temperatures in which water freezes at 0 degrees centigrade and boils at 100 degrees centigrade

centimeter ***noun*** a measure of length. There are 100 centimeters in a meter.

centipede ***noun*** a small animal like an insect, with a long thin body and very many legs

ceremony ***noun*** a formal public or religious event

charming ***adj.*** very pleasing or attractive

chuckled ***verb*** laughed quietly

circumstance ***noun*** the facts and events that affect what happens in a particular situation

civilization ***noun*** a society that has its own highly developed culture and way of life

clever ***adj.*** showing skill or intelligence

coins ***noun*** pieces of money made of metal

collaborate ***verb*** to work together (with someone), especially to create or produce something

collaboration ***noun*** the act of working with another person or group of people to create or produce something

collaborative ***adj.*** involving, or done by, several people or groups of people working together

comfortable ***adj.*** allowing you to feel relaxed

communicative ***adj.*** willing to talk or give information

complete ***adj.*** having or including all parts; with nothing missing

concert hall ***noun*** a building in which concerts are held

condenses ***verb*** changes or makes something change from a gas to a liquid

confusing ***adj.*** difficult to understand

connection ***noun*** an association or a relationship between two or more people or things

conservation ***noun*** the protection of the natural world

construction ***noun*** the act or method of building or making something

contribution ***noun*** something that you give or do together with others; the act of giving your share

cooperative ***adj.*** helpful; doing what someone asks you to do

copy ***verb*** [1] to write down something exactly as it is written somewhere else [2] to make a copy of a video, computer information, etc. [3] to do or try to do the same as someone else

cough ***verb*** to send air out of your throat and mouth with a sudden loud noise

countless ***adj.*** very many

courageous ***adj.*** having or showing courage

courthouse ***noun*** a building where courts of law and other government offices are

courtyard ***noun*** an area of ground, without a roof, that has walls or buildings around it, for example in a public building, or between houses or apartment buildings

creamy ***adj.*** thick and smooth like cream; containing a lot of cream

create ***verb*** to cause something new to happen or exist

creative ***adj.*** using skill or imagination to make or do new things

credible ***adj.*** that you can believe

crew ***noun*** all the people who work on a ship or plane

crops ***noun*** all the grain, fruit, vegetables, etc. that grow or are collected at one time or place

crunchy ***adj.*** hard and crisp, so that it makes a noise when you eat it or step on it

crush ***verb*** to press someone or something hard so that he/she/it is broken, damaged, or injured

crustaceans ***noun*** any creatures with a soft body that is divided into sections, and a hard outer shell. Most crustaceans live in water.

culture ***noun*** the customs, ideas, beliefs, etc. of a particular society or group of people

currency ***noun*** the system or type of money that a particular country uses

custom ***noun*** a way of behaving that a particular group or society has had for a long time

D

dam ***noun*** a wall built across a river to hold back the water and form a lake

damaged ***adj.*** spoiled, harmed, or broken

daring ***adj.*** involving or taking risks; brave

daytime ***noun*** the period of time after the sun rises and before it sets

decibel ***noun*** a measurement of how loud a sound is

deck ***noun*** [1] the top outside floor of a boat or ship [2] one of the floors of a ship, bus, etc.

decoration ***noun*** something that is added to something in order to make it look more attractive

decorative ***adj.*** attractive to look at; added to something to make it prettier

defend *verb* to act, especially to fight, to protect someone or something

delicate *adj.* fine or thin; easy to damage or break

delicious *adj.* having a very pleasant taste or smell

dental *adj.* connected with teeth

dependable *adj.* that can be trusted

design *verb* [1] to plan and make a drawing of how something will be made [2] to invent, plan, and develop something for a particular purpose

detective *noun* a person, especially a police officer, who tries to solve crimes or who investigates something

determined *adj.* having firmly decided to do something or to succeed, even if it is difficult

development *noun* the gradual growth of something so that it becomes more advanced, stronger, etc.

device *noun* a tool or piece of equipment made for a particular purpose

difficulty *noun* [1] a situation that is hard to deal with [2] something that is difficult to do or understand

distant *adj.* a long way away in space or time

dive *verb* to jump into water with your head first

diverse *adj.* very different from each other

dizzy *adj.* feeling as if everything is spinning around and that you might fall

dodo *noun* a large bird that could not fly and that no longer exists

doorbell *noun* a button on the outside of a house which you push when you want to ask the people inside to let you in

drawbridge *noun* a bridge that can be pulled up, for example to stop people from entering a castle or to allow ships to pass under it

drift *verb* to be carried or move along by wind or water

durable *adj.* that is able to last a long time

E

earring *noun* a piece of jewelry that is worn in or on the lower part of the ear

education *noun* the teaching or training of people, especially in schools, etc. to improve their knowledge and develop their skills

effective *adj.* producing the result that you want

elderly *adj.* (used about a person) old

elephant bird *noun* a very large bird that was not able to fly. Elephant birds are extinct.

embarrassed *adj.* feeling uncomfortable or shy because of something silly you have done, because people are looking at you, etc.

embarrassing *adj.* making you feel uncomfortable or shy

emerge *verb* to appear or come out from somewhere

enclose *verb* to surround something with a wall, fence, etc.

encouragement *noun* something you say that gives someone hope, support, or confidence

endangered *adj.* (used about animals, plants, etc.) in danger of disappearing from the world

endless *adj.* lasting for a long time and seeming to have no end

enough *determiner / pronoun* as much or as many of something as necessary

envious *adj.* feeling that you want something that someone else has

error *noun* a mistake

eventually *adv.* in the end; after a long time

exchange *verb* to give or receive something in return for something else

excitable *adj.* easily excited

exciting *adj.* causing strong feelings of pleasure or interest

existed *verb* was real; was found in the real world; was alive

exploit *verb* to use something or to treat someone unfairly for your own advantage

express *verb* to show something such as a feeling or an opinion by words or actions

extinct *adj.* (used about a type of animal, plant, etc.) no longer existing

F

fall off *phrasal verb* to become separated from something and drop down toward the ground

fang *noun* a long, sharp tooth of a dog, poisonous snake, etc.

fascinated *adj.* attracted or very interested in something

fascinating *adj.* extremely interesting and attractive

fend off *phrasal verb* to defend yourself from something or someone

fierce *adj.* [1] angry and aggressive [2] very strong

figures *noun* the shapes of bodies

filling *noun* the material that a dentist uses to fill a hole in a tooth

fishing rod *noun* a long thin stick with a long string and a hook on it for catching fish

float *verb* to stay or move gently on the surface of a liquid and not sink

flows *verb* moves in a smooth and continuous way (like water)

folded *verb* bent one part of something over another part in order to make it smaller, neater, etc.

foolish *adj.* silly; not sensible

footprint *noun* a mark that is left by a foot or a shoe

fortunate *adj.* lucky

fought *verb* past participle and past tense form of fight

fragile *adj.* easily damaged or broken

frightened *adj.* full of fear or worry

frightening ***adj.*** causing fear

function ***verb*** to work correctly; to be in action

G

gatehouse ***noun*** a house built at or over a gate, for example at the entrance to a park or a castle

gazed ***verb*** looked steadily for a long time

gear ***noun*** [1] the machinery in a vehicle that turns engine power into a movement forward or backward [2] a particular position of the gears on a bicycle, in a car, etc. that gives a particular range of speed and power

gigantic ***adj.*** extremely large

glacier ***noun*** a mass of ice that moves slowly across land

glide ***verb*** to move smoothly without noise or effort

gnaw ***verb*** (gnaw at or on something) to bite a bone, etc. many times

go back ***phrasal verb*** to return (to a place)

go on ***phrasal verb*** to continue

go up ***phrasal verb*** to increase

government ***noun*** the group of people who rule or control a country or state

grateful ***adj.*** feeling or showing thanks (to someone)

gravity ***noun*** extreme importance and a cause for worry

greedy ***adj.*** wanting more food, money, power, etc. than you really need

grind ***verb*** to crush something into very small pieces or into a powder, using a machine

grinning ***verb*** smiling broadly (so that you show your teeth)

grip ***verb*** to take and keep hold of someone or something firmly

growling ***verb*** (used about dogs and other animals) making a low noise in the throat to show anger or to give a warning

gums ***noun*** the hard pink parts of the mouth that hold the teeth

H

habitat ***noun*** the natural home of a plant or an animal

hall ***noun*** [1] a room or passage that leads to other rooms in a house or public building [2] a building or large room in which meetings, concerts, classes, etc. can be held

hand in ***phrasal verb*** to give something to someone in authority

handwriting ***noun*** a person's style of writing by hand

haul ***verb*** to pull or drag something with great effort

hear ***verb*** to receive sounds with your ears

herbivore ***noun*** an animal that only eats grass and plants

here ***adv.*** [1] in, at, or to the place where you are or which you are pointing to [2] used for introducing or drawing attention to someone or something

high ***adj.*** above the usual or normal level or amount

hill ***noun*** a high area of land that is not as high as a mountain

hook ***noun*** a curved piece of metal, plastic, etc. that is used for catching something or hanging something on

humorous ***adj.*** amusing or funny

hunter ***noun*** a person or animal that hunts

I

identify ***verb*** to recognize or be able to say who or what someone or something is

ill ***adj.*** not in good health; not well; sick

imitate ***verb*** to copy the behavior of someone or something

impatient ***adj.*** not able to wait for someone or something calmly; easily annoyed by someone or something that seems slow

imperfect ***adj.*** with mistakes or faults; not perfect

impolite ***adj.*** rude; not polite

impossible ***adj.*** not able to be done or to happen; not possible

improvement ***noun*** change which makes the quality or condition of something or someone better

inaccurate ***adj.*** not correct; not accurate

inactive ***adj.*** doing nothing; not active

inadequate ***adj.*** not sufficient; not good enough

incapable ***adj.*** not able to do something; not capable of something/doing something

incisor ***noun*** one of the eight sharp teeth at the front of the mouth that are used for biting

incomplete ***adj.*** having a part or parts missing; not total or complete

incorrect ***adj.*** not right or true; not correct

incredible ***adj.*** extremely good or extremely large

indicate ***verb*** [1] to show or point to something [2] to be or give a sign about something

indirect ***adj.*** not being the direct cause of something; not having a direct connection with something

inefficient ***adj.*** not working or producing results in the best way, so that time and money are wasted

inexpensive ***adj.*** low in price; not expensive

injure ***verb*** to harm or hurt a person, animal, or part of the body

injuries ***noun*** harm or hurt done to a person's or an animal's body, especially in an accident

innovative ***adj.*** introducing or using new ideas or ways of doing something

inspire ***verb*** to give someone a feeling of wanting and being able to do something good, create a work of art, etc.

inspiring *adj.* exciting and encouraging you to do or feel something

intruders *noun* people who enter a place without permission and often secretly

invisible *adj.* that cannot be seen

involuntary *adj.* done without wanting or meaning to

it's *contraction* short for "it is," "it has"

its *determiner* belonging to a thing, animal, etc.

J

jagged *adj.* rough with sharp points; not even

jaw *noun* either of the bones in your face that contain the teeth

jog *verb* to run slowly, especially as a form of exercise

jungles *noun* thick forests in a hot tropical country

L

ladle *verb* to serve food with a ladle (a large deep spoon with a long handle)

lap up *phrasal verb* (usually used about an animal) to drink something using the tongue

lend *verb* to allow someone to use something for a short time or to give someone money that must be paid back after a certain period of time

lie down *phrasal verb* to be or put yourself in a flat or horizontal position so that you can rest

lighthouse *noun* a tall building with a light at the top that guides ships or warns them of dangerous rocks, etc.

locate *verb* to find the exact position of someone or something

location *noun* a place or position

lodge *noun* the main building at a hotel in the country, where people stay, especially to do sports or outdoor activities

longed for *verb* wanted something very much

M

magnified *verb* made something look bigger than it really is

mammals *noun* animals of the type that give birth to live babies, not eggs, and feed their young on milk from their own bodies

marvelous *adj.* extremely good

massive *adj.* very big

measurement *noun* a size, amount, etc. that is found by measuring

mechanical *adj.* connected with, worked by, or produced by machines

migration *noun* the movement of large numbers of people, birds, or animals from one place to another

mill *noun* [1] a building that contains a large machine that is used for crushing grain into flour [2] a factory that is used for making certain kinds of material

miniature *adj.* very small; much smaller than usual

miscalculate *verb* to make a mistake in calculating or estimating (a situation or an amount, a distance, etc.)

miscommunication *noun* not communicating information that is correct or easy to understand

misdirect *verb* [1] to use something in a way that is not appropriate to a particular situation [2] to send someone or something in the wrong direction or to the wrong place

misjudge *verb* to form a wrong opinion of someone or something or to estimate something wrongly

misread *verb* to read or understand something wrongly

misremember *verb* to remember something wrongly

missing *adj.* lost, or not in the right or usual place

mission *noun* an important task or purpose that a person or group of people are sent somewhere to do

mistreat *verb* to behave badly or in a cruel way toward a person or animal

mistrust *verb* to have no confidence in someone or something because you think they may be harmful; to not trust someone or something

moat *noun* a deep hole that was dug around a castle and filled with water in order to protect the castle

molar *noun* one of the large teeth in the back of your mouth

molds *noun* hollow containers that you use to make things into a particular shape. You put a liquid substance into molds and wait for it to become solid (to set) in the same shape as the containers.

mountainous *adj.* having many mountains

mountain range *noun* a line of mountains

mouth-watering *adj.* (used about food) that looks or smells very good

mumble *verb* to speak quietly without opening your mouth enough so that people cannot really hear the words

munch *verb* to eat something in a noisy way, especially something crisp

muscles *noun* pieces of flesh inside the body which you can relax or make tight to produce movement

mutter *verb* to speak in a low, quiet, and sometimes rather angry voice that is difficult to hear

mysterious *adj.* that you do not know about or cannot explain

N

national park *noun* a large area of beautiful land that is protected by the federal government so that the public can enjoy it

naturalist *noun* a person who studies plants and animals

nervously *adv.* in a way that shows you are nervous or afraid

nutty *adj.* containing or tasting like nuts

O

obedient *adj.* doing what you are told to do

office ***noun*** a room or building where written work is done, especially work connected with a business

omnivore ***noun*** an animal that eats both plants and meat

owe ***verb*** to have to pay money to someone for something that he/she has done or given

P

paddle ***verb*** to move a small boat through water using a special type of short pole

paddles ***noun*** short poles that are wide at one or both ends and that you use for moving a small boat through water

padlock ***noun*** a type of lock that is used for fastening gates, bicycles, etc.

palace ***noun*** a large house that is or was the home of a king or queen

pay ***verb*** [1] to give someone money for something [2] to give the money that you owe for something

peak ***noun*** [1] the pointed top of a mountain [2] the highest level, value, rate, etc.

permanent ***adj.*** lasting for a long time or forever; that will not change

petrified ***adj.*** very frightened

pick up ***phrasal verb*** to take hold of and lift someone or something

pierce ***verb*** to make a hole in something with a sharp point

platform ***noun*** a flat, raised surface on which equipment stands

playwright ***noun*** a person who writes plays for the theater, TV, or radio

pleasing ***adj.*** giving pleasure

plod ***verb*** to walk slowly and in a heavy or tired way

poaching ***verb*** catching or killing birds, animals, or fish illegally, especially on someone else's land

pointy ***adj.*** with a point at one end

politely ***adv.*** in a polite way/in a way that shows respect for others

population ***noun*** a number of people who live in a particular place

portraits ***noun*** pictures, paintings, or photographs of a person

possessive ***adj.*** not wanting to share someone or something

powerful ***adj.*** very strong in a physical way

preservation ***noun*** keeping something in the same or in good condition

preserve ***verb*** to keep something safe or in good condition

preventable ***adj.*** that was or could be stopped from happening; unnecessary

preventing ***verb*** stopping something from happening or stopping someone from doing something

prevention ***noun*** the act of preventing something

prey ***noun*** an animal or bird that is killed and eaten by another animal or bird

print ***verb*** to produce a book, newspaper, etc.

process ***noun*** a series of actions that you do for a particular purpose

produce ***verb*** to cause something to happen

product ***noun*** a thing that is grown or produced, usually for sale

promote ***verb*** to encourage something; to help something to happen or develop

propel ***verb*** to move, drive, or push someone or something forward

propelling ***verb*** moving, driving, or pushing someone or something forward

protect ***verb*** to keep someone or something safe; to defend someone or something

protection ***noun*** (a way of) keeping someone or something safe so that he/she/it is not harmed or damaged

protective ***adj.*** that prevents someone or something from being damaged or harmed

provide ***verb*** to give something to someone who needs it or make something available for someone to use; to supply something

provides ***verb*** gives something to someone who needs it or makes something available for someone to use; supplies something

punishment ***noun*** the act of punishing or the state of being punished

put down ***phrasal verb*** to place something, for example on the floor, a table, etc.

put on ***phrasal verb*** to place clothes on your body

Q

quagga ***noun*** a type of zebra from South Africa with dark stripes on the front of its body. The quagga is extinct.

R

race ***verb*** to go very fast or to move someone or something very fast

ramparts ***noun*** high wide walls of stone or earth with a path on top, built around a castle, town, etc. to defend it

rare ***adj.*** not done, seen, happening, etc. very often

react ***verb*** to do or say something because of something that has happened or been said

released ***verb*** allowed someone or something to be free

remarkable ***adj.*** unusual and surprising in a way that people notice

reserve ***noun*** an area of land where the plants, animals, etc. are protected by law

resources ***noun*** a supply of something, a piece of equipment, etc. that is available for someone to use

rim ***noun*** an edge at the top or outside of something that is round

risky ***adj.*** dangerous; involving a chance that something bad could happen

rod ***noun*** a thin, straight piece of wood or metal

rotate *verb* to turn in circles around a central point; to make something do this

rough *adj.* not smooth or level

rudely *adv.* in a way that shows a lack of respect for other people and their feelings

runny *adj.* containing more liquid than is usual or than you expected

S

sanctuary *noun* a place where birds or animals cannot be hunted and are protected from danger

save *verb* to make or keep someone or something safe from death, loss, changes, etc.

scowl *verb* to look at someone or something in an angry way

seal *verb* to fill a hole or cover something so that air or liquid does not get in or out

sea wolf *noun* a type of large, black and white seal that was found in the Caribbean. Sea wolves are extinct.

set *noun* the painted background, furniture, etc. used in a play or movie

settle *verb* to go and live permanently in a new country, an area, a town, etc.

settlement *noun* a place that a group of people have built and live in, where few or no people lived before

shells *noun* hard coverings that protect eggs, nuts, and some animals

shelter *noun* a building or a structure that gives protection or cover, for example from danger, bad weather, or attack

shielded *verb* protected someone or something from danger or damage

shine *verb* to give out or to reflect light

showroom *noun* a type of store where products such as cars or furniture are displayed

shyly *adv.* in a way that shows nervousness around other people

signal *noun* a sign, an action or a sound that sends a particular message

silhouette *noun* the dark outline or black shape of something seen against a light background

silver *noun* a valuable gray-white metal that is used for making jewelry, coins, etc.

skidded *verb* moved or slid sideways

skyscraper *noun* a very tall building

slice *verb* to cut something into thin pieces

slope *noun* a piece of ground that has one end higher than the other, like the side of a hill

smooth *adj.* (of a liquid mixture) without lumps

sniffing *verb* breathing air in through the nose in a way that makes a sound, especially because you have a cold or you are crying

solvable *adj.* that could or can be solved

solve *verb* to find a way of dealing with a problem or difficult situation

spaceship *noun* a vehicle in which people can travel into space

spacious *adj.* having a lot of space or room; large in size

species *noun* a group of animals or plants that are very similar to each other and that can breed together

spend *verb* to give or pay money for something

spicy *adj.* containing spice

splash *verb* (to cause a liquid) to fly in drops and make someone or something wet

spoke *noun* one of the thin pieces of metal that connect the center of a wheel to the outside edge

spot *verb* to see or notice someone or something

sprint *verb* to run a short distance as fast as you can

square *noun* an open space in a town or city that has buildings all around it

squirm *verb* to move your body in a way which shows you are uncomfortable, bored, or embarrassed

stables *noun* buildings where horses are kept

stadium *noun* a large playing area with rows of seats around it

stage *noun* a raised floor in a theater or concert hall, etc. on which actors, musicians, etc. perform

stammer *verb* to speak with difficulty when someone is feeling nervous, repeating sounds or words and often stopping, before saying things correctly

stand up *phrasal verb* to rise to your feet from another position

staring *verb* looking at someone or something for a long time

starving *adj.* extremely hungry

steel *noun* a strong, hard metal that is made of a mixture of iron and carbon

steep *adj.* (of a slope, hill, etc.) rising or falling quickly, not gradually

stern *adj.* serious and often disapproving; expecting someone to obey you

sticky *adj.* made of or covered in a substance that sticks to things that touch it

stiffen *verb* [1] to make yourself or part of your body firm, straight, and still, especially because you are angry or frightened [2] (of part of the body) to become, or to make something become, difficult to bend or move

stirring *verb* moving a liquid or substance around, using a spoon or something similar

storing *verb* putting something somewhere and keeping it there to use later

stretch *verb* [1] to push out your arms, legs, etc. as far as possible [2] (used about a piece of land or water, etc.) to cover a large area

study for ***verb*** to spend time learning about a subject by reading, going to college, etc.

suffered ***verb*** [1] experienced something bad, for example pain, sadness, difficulty, etc. [2] became worse in quality

suitable ***adj.*** right or appropriate for a particular purpose or occasion

suitcase ***noun*** a case with flat sides and a handle, used for carrying clothes, etc. when you are traveling

supply ***verb*** to provide someone or something with something that they need or want, especially in large quantities

surprising ***adj.*** causing surprise

surrounded ***adj.*** having something or someone all around

survive ***verb*** [1] to continue to live or exist [2] to continue to live or exist despite a dangerous event or time

swift ***adj.*** quick or fast; happening without delay

T

tablets ***noun*** flat pieces of stone, clay, etc. that have words written on them, especially ones that have been fixed to a wall in memory of an important person or event

take off ***phrasal verb*** to remove something, especially clothes

take out ***phrasal verb*** to remove something from inside something else

tale ***noun*** [1] a story about events that are not real. [2] a report or description of someone or something that is not necessarily true

talk about ***verb*** to discuss something

teasing ***verb*** laughing at someone and making jokes about him/her

technology ***noun*** the scientific knowledge and/or equipment that is needed for a particular industry, etc.

tedious ***adj.*** boring and lasting for a long time

telecommunication ***noun*** the process of communicating over long distances by using electronic equipment, for example by radio or telephone, or the business of providing equipment and services to communicate in this way

telephone ***noun*** an electrical system for talking to someone in another house, town, country, etc. by speaking into a special piece of equipment

tempest ***noun*** a violent storm

tempting ***adj.*** attractive in a way that makes you want to do or have something

terrace ***noun*** a flat area of stone next to a house, restaurant, etc. where people can eat, sit in the sun, etc.

terrifying ***adj.*** making you feel frightened

territory ***noun*** an area that an animal has as its own

theater ***noun*** a building where you go to see plays, etc.

their ***determiner*** belonging to them

there ***adv.*** [1] used to show that something exists or happens [2] in, at, or to that place

think about ***verb*** to use your mind to consider something or to form connected ideas

though ***conjunction*** in spite of the fact that; although

threaten ***verb*** to warn that you may hurt, kill, or punish someone if he/she does not do what you want

thrilling ***adj.*** very exciting

through ***prep.*** from one end or side of something to the other

timid ***adj.*** easily frightened, shy

tools ***noun*** pieces of equipment that you use to help you do a particular type of job

toppling ***verb*** becoming unsteady and falling down, or causing someone to do this

tough ***adj.*** not easily broken or cut; very strong

tower ***noun*** a tall narrow building or part of a building

tracker ***noun*** a person who can find people or wild animals by following the marks that they leave on the ground

traction ***noun*** the force that stops something, for example the wheels of a vehicle, from sliding on the ground

trade ***verb*** to buy or sell goods or services

tradition ***noun*** a custom or belief that has continued from the past to the present

transfer ***verb*** to move, or to make someone or something move, from one place to another

transformed ***verb*** changed completely

transportation ***noun*** [1] moving someone or something from one place to another by vehicle [2] vehicles that you travel in

treat ***noun*** something that is very special or enjoyable

treatment ***noun*** the way you behave toward someone or deal with something

tremble ***verb*** to shake, for example because you are cold, frightened, weak, etc.

turrets ***noun*** small towers on the top of a large building

tusk ***noun*** one of the two very long pointed teeth of elephants and some other animals

U

underwater ***adj.*** existing, happening, or used below the surface of water

V

valley ***noun*** the flat land that lies between two lines of mountains or areas of higher ground, and which often has a river flowing through it

valuable ***adj.*** [1] worth a lot of money [2] very useful

vanished ***verb*** disappeared suddenly and completely

vapor ***noun*** a substance made of very small drops of liquid which hang together in the air like a cloud

vehicle ***noun*** something which transports people or things from place to place, especially on land, for example cars, bicycles, trucks, and buses

venom ***noun*** the poisonous liquid that snakes, etc. put into your body when they bite you

venomous ***adj.*** poisonous

villain ***noun*** an evil person, especially in a book, play, or movie

visible ***adj.*** that can be seen or noticed

voyage ***noun*** a long trip by ship or in space

W

wade ***verb*** to walk or stand with no shoes or socks in shallow water

warehouse ***noun*** a building where large quantities of products are kept before being sent to stores

water cycle ***noun*** a set of events in which water that falls from clouds as rain or snow lands on the ground or in oceans, lakes, etc. and is then heated by the sun and changed into very small drops of liquid that rise back into the air. These drops of liquid fall back onto the ground as rain or snow. This happens repeatedly in the same order.

wear down ***phrasal verb*** to become, or make something become, gradually smaller or smoother by continuously using or rubbing it

weird ***adj.*** strange and unusual or difficult to explain

wheelchair ***noun*** a chair with large wheels that a person who cannot walk can move around or be pushed in

whirring ***adj.*** making a continuous low sound

who's ***contraction*** short for "who is," "who has"

whose ***determiner, pronoun*** [1] (used in questions when you are asking who something belongs to) of whom? [2] of whom; of which

wildlife ***noun*** wild birds, plants, animals, etc.

winked ***verb*** closed and opened one eye very quickly, usually as a private signal to someone

wise ***adj.*** having or showing the knowledge or experience to make good or sensible decisions or judgments

woolly mammoth ***noun*** an animal like a large elephant covered with hair, that lived thousands of years ago. Woolly mammoths are extinct.

work for ***verb*** to do a job for a person or company, especially in order to earn money

Y

you're ***contraction*** short for "you are"

your ***determiner*** [1] belonging to or connected with the person or people being spoken to [2] belonging to or connected with people in general